THE MYSTICAL ROSE

THE MYSTICAL ROSE

THOUGHTS ON THE BLESSED VIRGIN
FROM THE WRITINGS OF
JOHN HENRY CARDINAL NEWMAN

Edited by Joseph Regina

Scepter Publishers

Princeton

The Mystical Rose by John Henry Cardinal Newman, edited and with a foreword by Joseph Regina, is reprinted with permission of St. Paul's (formerly St. Paul Publications), Middlegreen, Slough, SL3 6BT, United Kingdom. This 1996 edition is published by Scepter Publishers, Inc., P.O. Box 1270, Princeton, NJ 08542. *Nihil obstat:* Joannes M. T. Barton, S.T.D., L.S.D., *Censor deputatus. Imprimatur:* E. Morrogh Bernard, Vicar General, Westminster, March 31, 1955.

Library of Congress Cataloging-in-Publication Data

Newman, John Henry, 1801–1890.
   [Selections. 1996]
   The mystical rose : thoughts on the Blessed Virgin from the
writings of John Henry Cardinal Newman / edited by Joseph Regina
   p.   cm.
   Originally published: Staten Island, NY : St. Paul Publications,
1955.
   ISBN 0-933932-96-0 (pbk.)
   1. Mary, Blessed Virgin, Saint--Meditations. I. Regina, Joseph.
II. Title.
BT608.5.N48   1996
242'. 74--dc20   96–43091
                                                CIP

ISBN 0-933932-96-0

Publisher's Note

Cardinal Newman is considered one of the great English writers of the nineteenth century. To tamper with his prose, which, as editor Joseph Regina points out, is "suffused with vivid poetry," is considered akin to editing Shakespeare. Therefore we have refrained from trying to adapt his writing to the reading habits of the late twentieth century, with some small exceptions. Since today's readers may be daunted by the long sentences and paragraphs customary in nineteenth century writing, some of the longer paragraphs have been broken up and a period has occasionally replaced a colon or semicolon. Again, in a few places we have substituted a contemporary word or phrase when the one used has acquired a meaning that might lead to a misunderstanding of what Newman was saying. The clarity and insightfulness of Newman's thought, however, should more than make up for any difficulty caused by a somewhat unfamiliar style of rhetoric.

CONTENTS

viii

Foreword

MANY BOOKS are written every year to honor and spread the fame of the Mother of God, the Virgin Mary—prayer books and books of devotion which are intended to strengthen the faith and devotion of the faithful, and to inspire them with a loving trust in the power of her who has been called *omnipotentia supplex,* the all-powerful suppliant.

This book, *The Mystical Rose,* is not a new one. It is a collection of writings on the Virgin Mary by John Henry Cardinal Newman, who is considered by many to be the greatest religious thinker of the last century. It is a book both for study and devotion. There cannot be true devotion without ideas, without doctrine. Faith is objective, it is always and everywhere the same; devotion, on the other hand, is subjective and changes with times and places. The variety of devotions in various times and places has never even scratched the common faith of Catholics. It is characteristic of the Church to allow different devotions within the strict unity of the faith. Even after he became a Catholic, John Henry Newman could never completely understand some of the exterior forms of devotion practiced, for instance, in Italy; and yet no one could doubt Newman's living faith or his deep devotion to the Virgin Mary, to which the present work bears ample witness.

This book is intended to be a practical guide to help the faithful to spend a month or a period of time in union with Mary, the

Mother of God and our Mother—particularly the month of May, the most beautiful month of the year, "the month of promise and of joy."

In ancient times, the month of May was dedicated to sexual love with its rites in honor of Pan. The Church has done an astonishing sublime deed in transforming these pagan and sensual rites into the cult of the Most Pure Virgin! The month of May is the Spring of the year, and Mary is the Spring of Grace; the month of May is the month of flowers, and Mary is "The Flower," the Mystical Rose.

It was Pope Pius VII who, when he returned to Rome from his French exile in the month of May, approved, by means of two rescripts published in 1815 and 1822, the sweet custom of dedicating the month of May to our Lady, attaching at the same time, special indulgences to the practice. The whole Catholic world understood then that this beautiful devotion was full of meaning: it was like an offering of the first fruits to Mary.

The present work is composed of two parts, each of them consisting of extracts from Cardinal Newman's writings. The passages in the first part are taken from two of Newman's works. Up to page 44 the extracts are from the "Letter to Rev. E. B. Pusey," which is contained in Newman's *Difficulties of Anglicans,* Volume II. In this treatise, Newman seeks to show that Catholic teaching on Mary is based on the New Testament and on the Fathers of the ancient Church. Forms of devotion may have changed with the passage of time, but the faith has remained unchanged.

Then follow six extracts from Newman's *Discourses to Mixed Congregations,* 1849, which are remarkable for their form and language.

The second part of this volume is a sort of fine embroidery on the Litany of Loreto. It is a prose suffused with vivid poetry. It is taken entirely from Newman's work *Meditations and Devotions,* which appeared in 1893, three years after the great Cardinal's death. It fell to Father Neville, of the Birmingham Oratory, to publish it. It was perhaps Newman's intention that *Meditations and Devotions* should be part of a wider plan, part of a "Year of Devotions," like *The Christian Year* of his Anglican friend, John Keble; a year of devotions intended to sanctify the liturgical year. Various circumstances prevented Cardinal Newman from completing a work which would have been a true "manna" of devotion and edification for the faithful.

It seems hardly necessary to say anything about the well known personality of John Henry Cardinal Newman. This eminently religious man, who left Anglicanism for Catholicism after years of interior struggle; who devoted the whole of his life to the search for truth; who gave up everything for holiness—"holiness first"; who preferred holiness to peace—"holiness rather than peace"; who, though living in our world, had his thoughts always with the holy spirits in heaven; who saw in our earthly pilgrimage always and only a shadow of eternal life—"*ex umbris et imaginibus in veritatem*" (out of the shadows into reality): this man cannot be ignored in his most intimate distinguishing character, his holiness. Bishop Ullathorne of Birmingham, who knew him well, could say of him: "There is a saint in that man."

The thoughts on the Blessed Virgin collected in this book, show us Newman's sublime faith in Mary and devotion to her. The reader will draw from them new strength for his faith and a more tender and trusting love for our Heavenly Mother.

JOSEPH REGINA

Part I

The Belief of Catholics

I BEGIN by making a distinction which will help to remove some of the difficulty of my undertaking, as it presents itself to ordinary enquirers—the distinction between faith and devotion. I fully grant that devotion towards the Blessed Virgin has increased among Catholics with the progress of the centuries; but I do not agree that the Church's teaching concerning her has undergone a growth, for I believe that it has been in substance one and the same from the beginning.

By "faith" I mean the Creed and assent to the Creed; by "devotion" I mean such religious honors as belong to the objects of our faith, and the payment of those honors. Faith and devotion are as distinct in fact as they are in idea. We cannot, indeed, be devout without faith, but we may believe without feeling devotion. Of this phenomenon everyone has experience both in himself and in others, and we bear witness to it as often as we speak of realizing a truth or not realizing it. It may be illustrated, with more or less exactness, by matters which come before us in the world. For instance, a great author, or public man, may be acknowledged as such for a period of years; yet there may be an increase, an ebb and flow, in his popularity. And if he takes a lasting place in the minds of his countrymen, he may gradually grow into it, or suddenly be raised to it.

The idea of Shakespeare as a great poet has existed from a very early date in public opinion; and there were at least individuals in those days who understood him as well, and honored him as much, as the English people can honor him now.Yet, I think, there is a national devotion to him in this day such as never has been before. This has happened because, as education spreads throughout the country, there are more men able to enter into his poetical genius, and, among these, more capacity again for deeply and critically understanding him. And yet, from the first, he has exerted a great influence over the nation, as is seen from the fact that his phrases and sentences, more than can be numbered, have become almost proverbs among us.

And so again in philosophy, and in the arts and sciences, great truths and principles have sometimes been known and acknowledged for years; but, whether from feebleness of intellectual power in the recipients, or external circumstances of an accidental kind, they have not been turned to account. Thus the Chinese are said to have known of the properties of the magnet from time immemorial, and to have used it for land expeditions, yet not on the sea. Again, the ancients knew of the principle that water finds its own level, but seem to have made little application of their knowledge. And Aristotle was familiar with the principle of induction, yet it was left for Bacon to develop it into an experimental philosophy.

Illustrations such as these serve to convey that distinction between faith and devotion on which I am insisting. It is like the distinction between objective and subjective truth. The sun in the springtime will have to shine many days before it is able to melt the frost, open the soil, and bring out the leaves; yet it shines out from the first, though it makes its power felt but gradually. It is one and the same sun, though its influence day by day becomes greater. And so in the Catholic Church it is the one Virgin Mother, one and the same from first to last, and Catholics have ever acknowledged her. Yet, in spite of that acknowledgment, their devotion to her may be scanty in one time and place, and overflowing in another.

This distinction is forcibly brought home to a convert, as a peculiarity of the Catholic religion, on his first introduction to its worship. The faith is everywhere one and the same, but a large liberty is accorded to private judgment and inclination as regards matters of devotion. Any large church, with its various groups of people, will illustrate this. The church building itself is dedicated to Almighty God, under an invocation of the Blessed Virgin, or some particular saint; or again, of some mystery belonging to the Divine Name or the Incarnation; or of some mystery associated with the Blessed Virgin. Perhaps there are seven altars or more in it, and these again have their own saints. Then there is the feast proper to this or that day; and during the celebration of Mass, of all the worshippers who crowd around the priest, each has his own particular devotions, with which he follows the rite. No one interferes with his neighbor; agreeing, as it were, to differ, they pursue independently a common end, and by paths, distinct but converging, present themselves before God.

Then there are the confraternities attached to the church—of the Sacred Heart, or of the Precious Blood; associations of prayer for a good death, or for the repose of departed souls, or for the conversion of the heathen; devotions connected with the Rosary or scapular; not to speak of the great ordinary liturgy observed through the four seasons, or of the constant presence of the Blessed Sacrament, or of its ever-recurring rite of Benediction, and its extraordinary forty hours' Exposition. Or, again, look through any manual of prayer, and you at once will see both the number and variety of devotions that are open to individual Catholics to choose from, according to their religious taste and preferences.

Now these diversified modes of honoring God did not come to us in a day, or only from the apostles, they are the accumulations of centuries; and, as in the course of years, some of them spring up, so others decline and die. Some are local, in memory of some particular saint who happens to be the evangelist, or patron, or pride of the nation, or who lies entombed in the church or in the city where it is found. These devotions, necessarily, cannot have an earlier date than the saint's day of death or interment there.

The first of these sacred observances, long before such national memories, were the devotions paid to the apostles, then those which were paid to the martyrs. Yet there were saints nearer to our Lord than either martyrs or apostles; but these sacred persons were immersed and lost in the effulgence of his Glory, and because they did not manifest themselves, during their lifetime, in external works separate from him, it happened that for a long while they were less noticed. However, as time went on, the apostles, and then the martyrs, exerted less influence than before over the popular mind, and local saints, new creations of God's power, took their place, or the saints of some religious order. Then, as comparatively quiet times succeeded, the religious meditations of holy men and their quiet intercourse with heaven gradually exerted an influence, and permeated the Christian populace, by the instrumentality of preaching and by the ceremonial of the Church. Hence at length those luminous stars rose in the ecclesiastical heavens, which were of more august dignity than any which had preceded them. They were late in rising, for the very reason that they were so specially glorious.

Those names, I say, which at first sight might have been expected to enter earliest into the devotions of the faithful, with better reason might have been looked for at a later date, and actually were late in their coming. St. Joseph furnishes the most striking instance of this; here is the clearest of instances of the distinction between doctrine and devotion. Who, from his prerogatives and the testimony on which they come to us, had a greater claim to receive an early recognition among the faithful than he? A saint of Scripture, the foster-father of our Lord, he was an object of the universal and absolute faith of the Christian world from the first, yet devotion to him is of comparatively late date. When once it began, men seemed surprised that it had not been thought of before; and now, they hold him next to the Blessed Virgin in their religious affection and veneration. ("Letter to Rev. E. B. Pusey" in *Difficulties of Anglicans* [London, 1920], Vol. II, pp. 26–31.)

Mary, the Second Eve

WHAT IS the great rudimental teaching of Antiquity from its earliest date concerning her? By "rudimental teaching," I mean the *prima facie* view of her person and office, the broad outline laid down of her, the aspect under which she comes to us, in the writings of the Fathers. She is the Second Eve. Now let us consider what this implies. Eve had a definite, essential position in the first Covenant. The fate of the human race lay with Adam; he it was who represented us. It was in Adam that we fell; even though Eve had fallen, still, if Adam had stood, we should not have lost those supernatural privileges which were bestowed upon him as our first father.

Yet though Eve was not the head of the race, still, even as regards the race, she had a place of her own; for Adam, to whom was divinely committed the naming of all things, named her "the mother of all the living," a name surely expressive, not of a fact only, but of a dignity. But further, as she thus had her own general relation to the human race, so again she had her own special place, as regards its trial and its fall in Adam. In those primeval events, Eve had an integral share. "The woman, being seduced, was in the transgression." She listened to the Evil Angel; she offered the fruit to her husband, and he ate of it. She cooperated, not as an irresponsible instrument, but intimately and personally in the sin: she brought it about. As the history stands, she was a *sine qua non,* a positive, active cause of it; and she had her share in its punishment. In the sentence pronounced on her, she was recognized as a real agent in the temptation and its issue, and she suffered accordingly.

In that awful transaction there were three parties concerned—the serpent, the woman, and the man. And at the time of their sentence, an event was announced for a distant future in which the three same parties were to meet again, the serpent, the woman, and the man; but it was to be a second Adam and a second Eve, and the new Eve was to be the mother of the new Adam: "I will put enmity between thee and the woman and between thy seed and her seed." The seed of the woman is the Word Incarnate, and the woman, whose seed or son he is, is his mother Mary.

This interpretation, and the parallelism it involves, seem to me undeniable; but at all events, (and this is my point) the parallelism is the doctrine of the Fathers, from the earliest times. This being established, we are able, by the position and office of Eve in our fall, to determine the position and office of Mary in our restoration. (*Difficulties of Anglicans*, pp. 31-32.)

The Sanctity of Mary

MARY HOLDS, as the Fathers teach us, that office in our restoration which Eve held in our fall. Now, in the first place, what were Eve's endowments to enable her to enter upon her trial? She could not have stood again the wiles of the devil, though she was innocent and sinless, without the grant of a large grace. And this she had—a heavenly gift, which was over and above and additional to that nature of hers, which she received from Adam; a gift which had been given to Adam also before her, at the very time (as it is commonly held) of his original formation.

This is Anglican doctrine, as well as Catholic; it is the doctrine of Bishop Bull. He has written a dissertation on the point. He speaks of the doctrine which "many of the Schoolmen affirm, that Adam was created in grace that is, received a principle of grace and divine life from his very creation, or in the moment of the infusion of his soul, of which," he says, "for my own part I have little doubt." Again, he says, "It is abundantly manifest from the many testimonies alleged, that the ancient doctors of the Church did, with general consent, acknowledge that our first parents, in the state of integrity, had in them something more than nature, that is, were endowed with the divine principle of the Spirit, ordered to a supernatural felicity."

Now, taking this for granted, because I know that you and those who agree with you maintain it as well as we do, have you any intention to deny that Mary was as fully endowed as Eve? Is it any violent inference that she, who was to cooperate in the redemption of the world, was at least not less endowed with power from on high than she who, given as a helpmate to her husband, did in the event but cooperate with him for its ruin?

If Eve was raised above human nature by that indwelling moral gift which we call grace, is it rash to say that Mary had even a greater grace? And this consideration gives significance to the angel's salutation of her as "full of grace"—an interpretation of the original word which is undoubtedly the right one, as soon as we resist the common Protestant assumption that grace is a mere external approbation or acceptance, answering to the word "favor," whereas it is, as the Fathers teach, a real inward condition or superadded quality of soul. And if Eve had this supernatural inward gift given her from the first moment of her personal existence, is it possible to deny that Mary too had this gift from the very first moment of her personal existence? I do not know how to resist this inference. Well, this is simply and literally the doctrine of the Immaculate Conception. I say the doctrine of the Immaculate Conception is in its substance this, and nothing more or less than this (putting aside the question of degrees of grace). And it really does seem to me bound up in the doctrine of the Fathers that Mary is the Second Eve.

It is indeed to me a most strange phenomenon that so many learned and devout men stumble at this doctrine. I can only account for it by supposing that in matter of fact they do not know what we mean by the Immaculate Conception; and your volume (may I say it?) bears out my suspicion. It is a great consolation to have reason for thinking so—reason for believing that in some sort the persons in question are in the position of those great saints of former times, who are said to have hesitated about the doctrine, when they would not have hesitated at all if the word "conception" had been explained in that sense in which now it is universally received.

I do not see how anyone who holds with Bishop Bull the Catholic doctrine of the supernatural endowments of our first parents, has fair reason for doubting our doctrine about the Blessed Virgin. It has no reference whatever to her parents, but simply to her own person. It does but affirm that, together with the nature which she inherited from her parents, that is, her own nature, she had a superadded fullness of grace and that from the first moment of her existence.

Suppose Eve had stood the trial and not lost her first grace, and suppose she had eventually had children. Those children, from the first moment of their existence, would, through divine bounty, have received the same privilege that she had always had since she was taken from Adam's side; that is, they would have received what may be called an immaculate conception. They would then have been conceived in grace, as in fact they are conceived in sin. What is there difficult in this doctrine? What is there unnatural? Mary may be called, as it were, a daughter of Eve unfallen. You believe with us that St. John the Baptist had grace given to him three months before his birth, at the time that the Blessed Virgin visited his mother. And accordingly he was not immaculately conceived, because he was alive before grace came to him; but our Lady's case only differs from his in this respect, that to her the grace of God came, not just three months before her birth, but from the first moment of her being, as it had been given to Eve.

But it may be said: How does this enable us to say that she was conceived without original sin? If Anglicans knew what we mean by original sin, they would not ask the question. Our doctrine of original sin is not the same as the Protestant doctrine. "Original sin," with us, cannot be called sin in the mere ordinary sense of the word "sin." It is a term denoting Adam's sin as transferred to us, or the state to which Adam's sin reduces his children. But by Protestants it seems to be understood as sin, in much the same sense as actual sin. We, with the Fathers, think of it as something negative, Protestants as something positive. Protestants hold that it is a disease, a radical change of nature, an active poison internally corrupting the soul, infecting its primary elements, and disorganizing it. And they fancy that we ascribe a different nature from ours to the Blessed Virgin, different from that of her parents, and from that of fallen Adam. We hold nothing of the kind; we consider that in Adam she died, as all others do; that she was included, together with the whole race, in Adam's sentence; that she incurred his debt, as we do. But for the sake of him who was to redeem her and us upon the cross, to her the debt was remitted by anticipation. On her the sentence was not carried out, except indeed as regards her natural death, for she died when her time came, as others do.

All this we teach, but we deny that she had original sin. For by original sin we mean, as I have already said, something negative, that is, the deprivation of that supernatural unmerited grace which Adam and Eve had on their first formation—deprivation and the consequences of deprivation. Mary could not merit, any more than they, the restoration of that grace; but it was restored to her by God's free bounty, from the very first moment of her existence, and thereby, in fact, she never came under the original curse, which consisted in the loss of it. And she had this special privilege in order to fit her to become the Mother of her and our Redeemer, to fit her mentally, spiritually for it. So that, by the aid of the first grace, she might so grow in grace, that, when the angel came and her Lord was at hand, she might be "full of grace," prepared as far as a creature could be prepared to receive him into her bosom.

I have drawn the doctrine of the Immaculate Conception as an immediate inference, from the primitive doctrine that Mary is the Second Eve. The argument seems to me conclusive, and, if it has not been universally taken as such, this has come to pass because there has not been a clear understanding among Catholics what exactly was meant by the "Immaculate Conception." To many it seemed to imply that the Blessed Virgin did not die in

Adam, that she did not come under the penalty of the fall, that she was not redeemed, that she was conceived in some way inconsistent with the verse in the "Miserere" Psalm.

I cannot believe that the doctrine of the Immaculate Conception would have ever been opposed if controversy had in earlier days so clarified the subject as to make it plain to all that the doctrine meant nothing else than that in fact, in her case, the general sentence on mankind was not carried out; and that [this exemption was granted] by means of the indwelling in her of divine grace from the first moment of her being (and this is all the decree of 1854 has declared). An instinctive sentiment has led Christians jealously to put the Blessed Mary aside when sin comes into discussion. This is expressed in the well-known words of St. Augustine, All have sinned "except the Holy Virgin Mary, concerning whom, for the honor of the Lord, I wish no question to be raised at all, when we are treating of sins." These words, whatever St. Augustine's actual occasion of using them, certainly, in the spirit which they breathe, are well adapted to convey the notion that, though her parents had no privilege beyond other parents, she did not personally have any part in sin whatever. (*Difficulties of Anglicans,* pp. 44–50.)

The Dignity of Mary

HERE LET US suppose that our first parents had overcome in
their trial and had gained for their descendants forever the
full possession, as if by right, of the privileges which were
promised to their obedience—grace here and glory hereafter. Is
it possible that those descendants, pious and happy from age to
age in their temporal homes, would have forgotten their bene-
factors? Would they not have followed them in thought into the
heavens and gratefully commemorated them on earth? The history of the temptation, the craft of the serpent, their steadfast-
ness in obedience—the loyal vigilance, the sensitive purity of
Eve—the great issue, salvation wrought out for all generations
—would have been never from their minds, ever welcome to
their ears. This would have taken place from the necessity of our
nature.

Every nation has its mythical hymns and epics about its first
fathers and its heroes. The great deeds of Charlemagne, Alfred,
Coeur de Lion, Louis the Ninth, Wallace, Joan of Arc do not die;
and though they are gone from us, we make much of their names.
Milton's Adam, after his fall, understands the force of this law and
shrinks from the prospect of its operation.

> Who of all ages to succeed, but, feeling
> The evil on him brought by me, will curse
> My head? Ill fare our ancestor impure,
> For this we may thank Adam.

If this anticipation of the first man has not been fulfilled in the event, it is owing to the exigencies of our penal life, our state of perpetual change, and the ignorance and unbelief caused by the fall. Also because, fallen as we are, still from the hopefulness of our nature, we feel more pride in our national great men than dejection at our national misfortunes. Much more then in the great kingdom and people of God—the saints are ever in our sight, and not as mere ineffectual ghosts or dim memories, but as if present bodily in their past selves. It is said of them, "Their works do follow them"; what they were here, such are they in heaven and in the Church. As we call them by their earthly names, so we contemplate them in their earthly characters and histories. Their acts, callings, and relations below are types and anticipations of their present mission above.

Even in the case of our Lord himself, whose native home is the eternal heaven, it is said of him in his state of glory that he is "a priest forever"; and when he comes again, he will be recognized by those who pierced him as being the very same that he was on earth. The only question is whether the Blessed Virgin had a part, a real part, in the economy of grace, whether, when she was on earth, she secured by her deeds any claim on our memories. For, if she did, it is impossible we should put her away from us, merely because she is gone hence, and should not look at her still according to the measure of her earthly history, with gratitude and expectation.

If, as St. Irenaeus says, she acted the part of an advocate, a friend in need, even in her mortal life; if as St. Jerome and St. Ambrose say, she was on earth the great pattern of virgins; if she had a meritorious share in bringing about our redemption; if her maternity was gained by her faith and obedience; if her divine Son was subject to her; and if she stood by the cross with a mother's heart and drank in to the full those sufferings which it was her portion to gaze upon, it is impossible that we should not associate these characteristics of her life on earth with her present state of blessedness. And this surely she anticipated when she said in her hymn that all "generations should call me blessed."

I am aware that in thus speaking, I am following a line of thought that is rather a meditation than an argument in controversy, and I shall not carry it further. But still, before turning to other topics, it is to the point to enquire whether people's surprise, at our belief in the Blessed Virgin's present dignity, does not arise from the fact that most of them have never calmly considered her historical position in the Gospels, so as rightly to realize what that position imports. I do not claim for the generality of Catholics any greater powers of reflection upon the objects of their faith than Protestants commonly have. But, putting the run of Catholics aside, there is a sufficient number of religious men among us who, instead of expending their devotional energies (as so many serious Protestants do) on abstract doctrines, such as justification by faith only, or the sufficiency of Holy Scripture, employ themselves in the contemplation of Scripture facts, and bring out before their minds in a tangible form the doctrines involved in them and give such a substance and color to sacred history as to influence their brethren. And these brethren, though superficial themselves, are drawn by their Catholic instinct to accept conclusions which they could not indeed themselves have elicited, but which, when elicited, they feel to be true. However, it would be out of place to pursue this course of reasoning here; and instead of doing so, I shall take what perhaps you may think a very bold step—I shall find the doctrine of our Lady's present exaltation in Scripture.

I mean to find it in the vision of the Woman and Child in the twelfth chapter of the Book of Revelation. Now here two objections will be made to me at once; first that such an interpretation is but poorly supported by the Fathers, and secondly that in ascribing such a picture of the Madonna (as it may be called) to the Apostolic Age, I am committing an anachronism.

As to the former of these objections, I answer as follows: Christians have never gone to Scripture for proof of their doctrines until there was actual need from the pressure of controversy. If in those times the Blessed Virgin's dignity was unchallenged on all hands as a matter of doctrine, Scripture, as far as its argumentative matter was concerned, was likely to remain a sealed book to them. Thus, to take an instance in point; the Catholic party in the Anglican Church (say, the Nonjurors), unable by their theory of religion simply to take their stand on tradition, and searching for proof of their doctrines, had their eye sharpened to scrutinize and to understand in many places the letter of Holy Scripture, which to others brought no instruction. And the peculiarity of their interpretation is this—that these have in themselves great logical cogency yet are but faintly supported by patristical commentators.

As to the second objection which I have supposed, so far from allowing it, I consider that it is built upon a mere imaginary fact, and that the truth of the matter lies in the very contrary direction. The Virgin and Child is not a mere modern idea; on the contrary, it is represented again and again, as every visitor to Rome is aware, in the paintings of the Catacombs. Mary is there drawn with the Divine Infant in her lap, and she with hands extended in prayer, he with his hand in the attitude of blessing. No representation can more forcibly convey the doctrine of the high dignity of the Mother and, I will add, of her influence with her Son.

Why should the memory of his time of subjection be so dear to Christians and so carefully preserved? The only question to be determined is the precise date of these remarkable monuments of the first age of Christianity. That they belong to the centuries of what Anglicans call the "undivided Church" is certain; but lately investigations have been pursued which place some of them at an earlier date than anyone anticipated as possible.

I am not in a position to quote at length from the works of the Cavaliere de Rossi, who has thrown so much light upon the subject; but I have his *Imagini Scelte,* published in 1863, and they are sufficient for my purpose. In this work he has given us from the Catacombs various representations of the Virgin and Child; the latest of these belong to the early part of the fourth century, but the earliest he believes to date from the very age of the apostles. He comes to this conclusion from the style and the skill of its composition and from the history, locality, and existing inscriptions of the subterranean area in which it is found. However, he does not go so far as to insist upon so early a date; yet the utmost concession he makes is to refer the painting to the era of the first Antonines, that is to a date within half a century of the death of St. John.

In controversy with Protestants you could certainly use the traditional doctrine of the Church in early times as an explanation of a particular passage of Scripture, or at least as a suggestion, or as a defense, of the sense which you may wish to put upon it, quite apart from the question whether your interpretation itself is directly traditional. In the same way it is lawful for me, though I have not the positive words of the Fathers on my side, to shelter my own interpretation of the apostle's vision in the Book of Revelation under the fact of the extant pictures of Mother and Child in the Roman Catacombs.

Again, there is another principle of Scripture interpretation which we hold as well as you. That is, when we speak of a doctrine being contained in Scripture, we do not necessarily mean that it is contained there in direct categorical terms, but that there is no satisfactory way of accounting for the language and expressions of the sacred writers, concerning the subject matter in question, except to suppose that they held concerning it the opinion which we hold—that they would not have spoken as they have spoken unless they held it. For myself I have always felt the truth of this principle, as regards the Scripture proof of the Holy Trinity. I would not have discovered that doctrine in the sacred text without previous traditional teaching. But, when once it is suggested from without, it commends itself as the one true interpretation, from its appositeness—because no other view of doctrine, which can be ascribed to the inspired writers, so happily solves the obscurities and seeming inconsistencies of their teaching. And now to apply what I have been saying to the passage in the Book of Revelation.

If there is an apostle on whom our eyes would be fixed, as likely to teach us about the Blessed Virgin, it is St. John, to whom she was committed by our Lord on the cross—with whom, as tradition goes, she lived at Ephesus till she was taken away. This anticipation is confirmed; for, as I have said above, one of the earliest and fullest of our informants concerning her dignity, as being the Second Eve, is Irenaeus, who came to Lyons from Asia Minor and had been taught by the immediate disciples of St. John. The apostle's vision is as follows:

"A great sign appeared in heaven: A woman clothed with the sun, and the moon under her feet; and on her head a crown of twelve stars. And being with child, she cried travailing in birth, and was in pain to be delivered. And there was seen another sign in heaven; and behold a great red dragon . . . And the dragon stood before the woman who was ready to be delivered, that, when she should be delivered, he might devour her son. And she brought forth a man-child, who was to rule all nations with an iron rod; and her son was taken up to God and to his throne. And the woman fled into the wilderness." Now I do not deny of course that under the image of the woman, the Church is signified; but what I would maintain is this, that the holy apostle would not have spoken of the Church under this particular image unless there had existed a Blessed Virgin Mary who was exalted on high and the object of veneration of all the faithful.

No one doubts that the "man-child" spoken of is an allusion to our Lord: why then is not the "woman" an allusion to his

Mother? This surely is the obvious sense of the words. Of course they have a further sense also, which is the scope of the image; doubtless the child represents the children of the Church, and doubtless the woman represents the Church. This, I grant, is the real or direct sense, but what is the sense of the symbol under which that real sense is conveyed? I answer, they are not personifications but persons. This is true of the child, therefore it is true of the woman.

But again, not only mother and child, but a serpent is introduced into the vision. Such a meeting of man, woman, and serpent has not been found in Scripture since the beginning of Scripture, and now it is found at its end. Moreover, in the passage in the Book of Revelation, as if to supply, before Scripture came to an end, what was wanting in its beginning, we are told, and for the first time, that the serpent in Paradise was the evil spirit. If the dragon of St. John is the same as the serpent of Genesis, and the man-child is "the seed of the woman," why is not the woman herself she whose seed the man-child is? And, if the first woman is not an allegory, why is the second? If the first woman is Eve, why is not the second Mary?

But this is not all. The image of the woman, according to general Scripture usage, is too bold and prominent for a mere personification. Scripture is not fond of allegories. We have indeed frequent figures there, as when the sacred writers speak of the arm or sword of the Lord. So, too, when they speak of Jerusalem or Samaria in the feminine, or of the Church as a bride or as a vine. But they are not much given to dressing up abstract ideas or generalizations in personal attributes. This is the classical rather than the Scriptural style. Xenophon places Hercules between Virtue and Vice, represented as women; Aeschylus introduces into his drama Force and Violence; Virgil gives personality to public rumor or Fame, and Plautus to Poverty.

So, on monuments done in the classical style, we see virtues, vices, rivers, renown, death and the like turned into human figures

of men and women. Certainly I do not deny there are some instances of this method in Scripture, but I say that such poetical
compositions are strikingly unlike its usual method. Thus, we at
once feel the difference from Scripture when we betake ourselves
to the Pastor of Hermas (a second century Christian writing) and
find the Church a woman; to St. Methodius (third century) and
find Virtue a woman; and to St. Gregory Nazianzen's poem (fourth
century) and find Virginity, again a woman. Scripture deals with
types rather than personifications. Israel stands for the chosen
people, David for Christ, Jerusalem for heaven. Consider the remarkable representations, dramatic I may call them, in Jeremiah,
Ezekiel, and Hosea: predictions, threatenings, and promises are
acted out by those prophets. Ezekiel is commanded to shave his
head and to divide and scatter his hair; and Ahias tears his garment
and gives ten out of twelve parts of it to Jereboam. So, too, the
structure of the imagery in the Book of Revelation is not a mere
allegorical creation, but is founded on the Jewish ritual.

In like manner our Lord's bodily cures are visible types of the
power of his grace on the soul, and his prophecy of the last day is
conveyed under that of the fall of Jerusalem. Even his parables are
not simply ideal but relations of occurrences which did or might
take place, under which was conveyed a spiritual meaning. The description of Wisdom in the Proverbs and other sacred books has
brought out the instinct of commentators in this respect. They felt
that Wisdom could not be a mere personification, and they determined that it was our Lord. And the later-written of these books,
by their own more definite language, warranted that interpretation. Then, when it was found that the Arians used it in derogation of our Lord's divinity, still, unable to tolerate the notion of a
mere allegory, commentators applied the description to the
Blessed Virgin.

Coming back, then, to the vision in the Book of Revelation,
I ask, If the Woman ought to be some real person, who can it be

whom the apostle saw, and intends, and delineates, but that same
Great Mother to whom the chapters in the Proverbs are accom-
modated? And let it be observed, moreover, that in this passage,
from the allusion made in it to the history of the fall, Mary may
be said still to be represented under the character of the Second
Eve. I make a further remark: it is sometimes asked, Why do not
the sacred writers mention our Lady's greatness? I answer, she was,
or may have been alive, when the apostles and evangelists wrote;
there was just one book of Scripture certainly written after her
death, and that book does (so to say) canonize and crown her.

But if all this be so, if it is really the Blessed Virgin whom
Scripture represents as clothed with the sun, crowned with the
stars of heaven, and with the moon as her footstool, what height
of glory may we not attribute to her? And what are we to say of
those who, through ignorance, run counter to the voice of Scripture, to the testimony of the Fathers, to the traditions of East and
West, and speak and act contemptuously towards her whom the
Lord delighteth to honor? (*Difficulties of Anglicans*, pp. 50–61.)

Mary, the Mother of God

Now I have said all I mean to say on what I have called the rudimental teaching of Antiquity about the Blessed Virgin; but after all, I have not insisted on the highest view of her prerogatives, which the Fathers have taught us. You, my dear friend, who know so well the ancient controversies and Councils, may have been surprised why I should not have yet spoken of her as the Theotokos [Mother of God]; but I wished to show on how broad a basis her dignity rests, independent of that wonderful title. And again I have been loath to enlarge upon the force of a word, which is rather matter for devotional thought than for polemical dispute. However, I might as well not write to you at all, as altogether be silent upon it.

It is, then, an integral portion of the faith fixed by Ecumenical Council, a portion of it which you [Anglicans] hold as well as I, that the Blessed Virgin is Theotokos, Deipara, or Mother of God. And this word, when thus used, carries with it no admixture of rhetoric, no taint of extravagant affection—it has nothing else but a well-weighed, grave, dogmatic sense, which corresponds and is adequate to its sound. It intends to express that God is her son, as truly as any one of us is the son of his own mother. If this be so, what can be said of any creature whatever, which may not be said of her? What can be said too much, so long as it does not compromise the attributes of the Creator? He indeed might have created a being more perfect, more admirable, than she is; he might have endowed that being, so created, with a richer grant of grace, of power, of

24

blessedness, but in one respect she surpasses all possible creations—that she is Mother of her Creator.

It is this awe inspiring title which both illustrates and connects together the two prerogatives of Mary on which I have been lately enlarging, her sanctity and her greatness. It is the issue of her sanctity; it is the origin of her greatness. What dignity can be too great to attribute to her who is as closely bound up, as intimately one, with the Eternal Word, as a mother is with a son? What fullness and redundance of grace, what exuberance of merits must have been hers, when once we admit the supposition, which the Fathers justify, that her Maker really did regard those merits, and take them into account, when he condescended "not to abhor the Virgin's womb"? Is it surprising then that on the one hand she should be immaculate in her conception? Or on the other that she should be honored with an Assumption and exalted as a queen with a crown of twelve stars, with the rulers of day and night to do her service? Men sometimes wonder that we call her Mother of life, of mercy, of salvation; what are all these titles compared to that one name, Mother of God?

I shall say no more about this title here. It is scarcely possible to write of it without diverging into a style of composition unsuited to a letter; so I will but refer to the history and to instances of its use.

The title of Theotokos, as ascribed to the Blessed Mary, begins with ecclesiastical writers of a date hardly later than that at which we read of her as the Second Eve. It first occurs in the works of Origen (185–254), but he, witnessing for Egypt and Palestine, witnesses also that it was in use before his time; for, as [the early Christian writer] Socrates informs us, he "interpreted how it was to be used, and discussed the question at length." Within two centuries of his time (431), in the General Council held against Nestorius, it was made part of the formal dogmatic teaching of the Church. At that time, Theodoret, who from his party connections might have been supposed disinclined to its solemn recognition, owned that "the ancient and more than ancient heralds of the orthodox faith taught the use of the term according to the apostolic tradition."

At the same date John of Antioch, the temporary protector of Nestorius, whose heresy lay in the rejection of the term, said, "This title no ecclesiastical teacher has put aside. Those who have used it are many and eminent; and those who have not used it, have not attacked those who did." Alexander again, one of the fiercest partisans of Nestorius, witnesses to the use of the word, though he considers it dangerous. "That in festive solemnities," he says, "or in preaching or teaching, 'Theotokos' should be unguardedly said by the orthodox without explanation is no blame, because such statements were not dogmatic, not said with evil meaning."

If we look for those Fathers, in the interval between Origen and the Council, to whom Alexander refers as using the term, we find among them no less names than Archelaeus of Mesopotamia, Eusebius of Palestine, Alexander of Egypt, in the third century; in the fourth, Athanasius, who uses it many times with emphasis, Cyril of Palestine, Gregory of Nyssa and Gregory Nazianzen of Cappadocia, Antiochus of Syria, and Ammonius of Thrace—not to refer to the Emperor Julian who, having no local or ecclesiastical domicile, is a witness for the whole of Christendom. Another and earlier emperor, Constantine, in his speech before the assembled Bishops at Nicaea, uses the still more explicit title of the "Virgin Mother of God"; which is also used by Ambrose of Milan, and by Vincent and Cassian in the south of France, and then by St. Leo.

So much for the term; it would be tedious to produce the passages of authors who, using or not using the term, convey the idea. "Our God was carried in the womb of Mary," says Ignatius, who was martyred A.D. 106. "The Word of God," says Hippolytus, "was carried in that Virgin frame." "The Maker of all," says Amphilochius, "is born of a Virgin." "She did compass without circumscribing the

Sun of justice—the Everlasting is born," says Chrysostom. "God dwelt in the womb," says Proclus. "When thou hearest that God speaks from the bush," asks Theodotus, "in the bush seest thou not the Virgin?" Cassian says, "Mary bore her Author." "The One God only-begotten," says Hilary, "is introduced into the womb of a Virgin." "The Everlasting," says Ambrose, "came into the Virgin." "The closed gate," says Jerome, "by which alone the Lord God of Israel enters, is the Virgin Mary." "That man from heaven," says Capriolus, "is God conceived in the womb." "He is made in thee," says St. Augustine, "who made thee."

This being the faith of the Fathers about the Blessed Virgin, we need not wonder that it should in no long time be transmuted into devotion. No wonder if their language should become unmeasured, when so great a term as "Mother of God" had been formally set down as the safe limit of it. No wonder if it should be stronger and stronger as time went on, since only in a long period could the fullness of its import be exhausted. And in matter of fact, and as might be anticipated (with the few exceptions which I have noted above, and which I am to treat of below), the current of thought in those early ages did uniformly tend to make much of the Blessed Virgin and to increase her honors, not to circumscribe them. Little jealousy was shown of her in those times; but, when any such niggardliness of affection occurred, then one Father or other fell upon the offender with zeal, not to say fierceness.

Thus, St. Jerome inveighs against Helvidius; thus, St. Epiphanius denounces Apollinaris; St. Cyril, Nestorius; and St. Ambrose, Bonosus. On the other hand, each successive insult offered her by individual adversaries did but bring out more fully the intimate sacred affection with which Christendom regarded her. "She was alone and wrought the world's salvation and conceived the redemption of all," says Ambrose. "She had so great grace, as not only to preserve virginity herself, but to confer it on those whom she visited."

"She is the rod out of the stem of Jesse," says St. Jerome, "and the eastern gate through which the High Priest alone goes in and out, which still is ever shut." "She is the wise woman," says Nilus, who "hath clad believers, from the fleece of the Lamb born of her, with the clothing of incorruption, and delivered them from their spiritual nakedness." "She is the Mother of life, of beauty, of majesty, the morning star," according to Antiochus. "The mystical new heavens," "the heavens carrying the Divinity," "the fruitful vine," "by whom we are translated from death unto life," according to St. Ephrem. "The manna which is delicate, bright, sweet, and virgin, which, as though coming from heaven, has poured down on all the people of the churches a food pleasanter than honey," according to St. Maximus.

Basil of Seleucia says that, "she shines out above all the martyrs as the sun above the stars, and that she mediates between God and men." "Run through all creation in your thought," says Proclus, "and see if there be one equal or superior to the Holy Virgin, Mother of God." "Hail, Mother, clad in light, of the light which sets not," says Theodotus, or someone else at Ephesus; "hail all undefiled Mother of holiness; hail, most pellucid fountain of the life-giving stream." And St. Cyril, too, at Ephesus, "Hail, Mary, Mother of God, majestic common treasure of the whole world, the lamp unquenchable, the crown of virginity, the scepter of orthodoxy, the indissoluble temple, the dwelling of the Illimitable, Mother and Virgin, through whom he in the holy Gospels is called blessed who cometh in the name of the Lord ... through whom the Holy Trinity is sanctified ... through whom angels and archangels rejoice, devils are put to flight ... and the fallen creature is received up into the heavens, etc., etc." Such is but a portion of the panegyrical language which St. Cyril used in the third Ecumenical Council. (*Difficulties of Anglicans*, pp. 61–67.)

Mary's Intercessory Power

I MUST NOT close my review of Catholic doctrine concerning the Blessed Virgin without directly speaking of her intercessory power, though I have incidentally made mention of it already. It is the immediate result of two truths, neither of which you dispute—first, that "it is good and useful," as the Council of Trent says, "suppliantly to invoke the saints and to have recourse to their prayers"; and secondly, that the Blessed Mary is singularly dear to her Son and singularly exalted in sanctity and glory. However, at the risk of becoming didactic, I will state somewhat more fully the grounds on which it rests.

To a candid pagan it must have been one of the most remarkable points of Christianity, on its first appearance, that the observance of prayer formed so vital a part of its organization. Though its members were scattered all over the world, and its rulers and subjects had so little opportunity of unified action, yet they, one and all, found the solace of spiritual intercourse and a real bond of union, in the practice of mutual intercession. Prayer indeed is the very essence of all religion, but in the heathen religions it was either public or personal. It was either a state ordinance or a selfish expedient for the attainment of certain tangible, temporal goods. Very different from this was its exercise among Christians, who were thereby knit together in one body, different, as they were, in race, rank, and habits, distant from each other in country, and helpless amid hostile populations. Yet it proved sufficient for its purpose. Christians could not correspond; they could not combine; but they could pray for one another. Even their public prayers partook of this character of intercession. For to pray for the welfare of the whole Church was in fact a prayer for all the classes of men and all the individuals of which it was composed.

It was in prayer that the Church was founded. For ten days all the apostles "persevered with one mind in prayer and supplication, with the women, and Mary the Mother of Jesus, and with his brethren." Then again at Pentecost "they were all with one mind in one place"; and the converts then made are said to have "persevered in prayer." And when, after a while, St. Peter was seized and put in prison with a view to being put to death, "prayer was made without ceasing" by the Church of God for him; and, when the angel released him, he took refuge in a house "where many were gathered together in prayer."

We are so accustomed to these passages as hardly to be able to do justice to their singular significance; and they are followed up by various passages of the apostolic epistles. St. Paul enjoins his brethren to "pray with all prayer and supplication at all times in the Spirit, with all instance and supplication for all saints," to "pray in every place," "to make supplication, prayers, intercessions, giving of thanks, for all men." And in his own person he "ceases not to give thanks for them, commemorating them in his prayers," and "always in all his prayers making supplication for them all with joy." Now, was this spiritual bond to cease with life? Or had Christians similar duties to their brethren departed? From the witness of the early ages of the Church, it appears that they had. You, and those who agree with you, would be the last to deny that they were then in the practice of praying, as for the living, so for those also who had passed into the intermediate state between earth and heaven. Did the sacred communion extend further still, on to the inhabitants of heaven itself? Here too you agree with us, for you have adopted in your volume the words of the Council of Trent which I have quoted above. But now we are brought to a higher order of thought.

It would be preposterous to pray for those who are already in glory, but at least they can pray for us, and we can ask their prayers. In the Book of Revelation at least, angels are introduced both sending us their blessing and offering up our prayers before the Divine Presence. We read there of an angel who "came and stood before the altar, having a golden censer"; and "there was given to him much incense, that he should offer of the prayers of all the saints upon the golden altar which is before the throne of God." On this occasion, surely the angel performed the part of a great intercessor or mediator above for the children of the Church Militant below.

Again, in the beginning of the same book, the sacred writer goes so far as to speak of "grace and peace" coming to us, not only from the Almighty, "but from the seven spirits that are before his throne," thus associating the Eternal with the ministers of his mercies. And this carries us on to the remarkable passage of St. Justin, one of the earliest Fathers, who, in his "Apology," says, "To him (God), and his Son who came from him and taught us these things, and the host of the other good angels who follow and resemble him, and the prophetic spirit, we pay veneration and homage." Further, in the Epistle to the Hebrews, St. Paul introduces, not only angels, but "the spirits of the just" into the sacred communion: "Ye have come to Mount Zion, to the heavenly Jerusalem, to myriads of angels, to God the Judge of all, to the spirits of the just made perfect, and to Jesus the Mediator of the New Testament." What can be meant by having "come to the spirits of the just," unless in some way or other, they do us good, whether by blessing or aiding us? That is, in a word, to speak correctly, by praying for us, for it is surely by prayer that the creature above is able to bless and aid the creature below.

Intercession thus being a first principle of the Church's life, next it is certain again that the vital force of that intercession, as an availing power, is (according to the will of God) sanctity. This seems to be suggested by a passage of St. Paul in which the Supreme Intercessor is said to be "the Spirit"—"the Spirit himself maketh intercession for us; he maketh intercession for the saints according to God." And, indeed, the truth thus implied, is expressly brought out for us in other parts of Scripture, in the form both of doctrine and of example. The words of the man born blind speak the common sense of nature: "If any man be a worshipper of God, him he heareth." And apostles confirm them: "The prayer of a just man availeth much," and "whatever we ask, we receive, because we keep his commandments." Then, for example, we read of the Almighty's revealing to Abraham and Moses beforehand, his purposes of wrath, in order that they by their intercessions might avert its execution. To the friends of Job it was said: "My servant Job shall pray for you; his face I will accept." Elias by his prayer shut and opened the heavens.

Elsewhere we read of "Jeremiah, Moses, and Samuel"; and of "Noah, Daniel, and Job," as being great mediators between God and his people. One instance is given us which testifies the continuance of this high office beyond this life. Lazarus, in the parable, is seen in Abraham's bosom. It is usual to pass over this striking passage with the remark that it is a Jewish mode of speech; whereas, Jewish belief or not, it is recognized and sanctioned by our Lord himself. What do Catholics teach about the Blessed Virgin more wonderful than this? If Abraham, not yet ascended on high, had charge of Lazarus, what offense is it to affirm the like of her, who was not merely as Abraham, "the friend," but was the very "Mother of God"?

It may be added, that, though, if sanctity was wanting, it availed nothing for influence with our Lord to be one of his company, still, as the Gospel shows, he on various occasions actually did allow those who were near him to be the channels of introducing supplicants to him, or of gaining miracles from him as in the instance of the miracles of the loaves. And if on one occasion, he

seems to repel his Mother, when she told him that wine was wanting for the guests at the marriage feast, it is obvious to remark on
it, that, by saying that she was then separated from him ("What
have I to do with thee?") because his hour was not yet come; he
implied that when that hour was come, such separation would be
at an end. Moreover, in fact he did at her intercession work the
miracle to which her words pointed.

I consider it impossible then, for those who believe the
Church to be one vast body in heaven and on earth, in which
every holy creature of God has his place, and of which prayer is
the life, when once they recognize the sanctity and dignity of the
Blessed Virgin, not to perceive immediately that her office above
is one of perpetual intercession for the faithful militant, and that
our very relation to her must be that of clients to a patron, and
that, in the eternal enmity which exists between the woman and
the serpent, while the serpent's strength lies in being the Tempter,
the weapon of the Second Eve and Mother of God is prayer.

As then these ideas of her sanctity and dignity gradually pen-
etrated the mind of Christendom, so did that of her intercessory
power follow close upon them and with them. From the earliest
times that mediation is symbolized in those representations of
her with uplifted hands, which, whether in plaster or in glass, are
still extant in Rome—that Church, as St. Irenaeus says, with
which "every church, that is, the faithful from every side, must
agree, because of its more powerful principality"; "into which,"
as Tertullian adds, "the apostles poured out, together with their
blood, their whole doctrine." As far indeed as existing documents
are concerned, I know of no instance to my purpose earlier than
A.D. 234, but it is a very remarkable one; and, though it has been
often quoted in the controversy, an argument is not weaker for
frequent use.

St. Gregory of Nyssa, then, a native of Cappadocia in the
fourth century, relates that his namesake, Bishop of Neo-Caesarea

in Pontus, surnamed Thaumaturgus, in the century preceding, shortly before he was called to the priesthood, received in a vision a creed, which is still extant, from the Blessed Mary at the hands of St. John. The account runs thus: he was deeply pondering theological doctrine, which the heretics of the day depraved. "In such thoughts," says his namesake of Nyssa, "he was passing the night, when one appeared, as if in human form, aged in appearance, saintly in the fashion of his garments, and very venerable both in grace of countenance and general mien. Amazed at the sight, he started from his bed and asked who it was and why he came; but, at the other calming the perturbation of his mind with his gentle voice, and saying he had appeared to him by divine command on account of his doubts, in order that the truth of the orthodox faith might be revealed to him, he took courage at the word and regarded him with a mixture of joy and fright. Then, on his stretching his hand straight forward and pointing with his fingers at something on one side, he followed with his eyes the extended hand, and saw another appearance opposite to the former, in shape of a woman, but more than human. . . .

"When his eyes could not bear the apparition, he heard them conversing together on the subject of his doubts; and thereby not only gained a true knowledge of the faith, but learned their names, as they addressed each other by their respective appellations. And thus he is said to have heard the person in woman's shape bid 'John the Evangelist' disclose to the young man the mystery of godliness; and he answered that he was ready to comply in this matter with the wish of the 'Mother of the Lord,' and enunciated a formulary, well-turned and complete, and so vanished. He, on the other hand, immediately committed to writing that divine teaching of his mystagogue, and henceforth preached in the Church according to that form, and bequeathed to posterity, as an inheritance, that heavenly teaching, by means of which his people are instructed down to this day, being preserved from all heretical evil." He proceeds to rehearse the creed thus given: "There is one God, Father of a Living Word," etc. Bull, after quoting it in his work on the Nicene faith, alludes to the history of its origin, and adds, "No one should think it incredible that such a providence should befall a man whose whole life was conspicuous for revelations and miracles, as all ecclesiastical writers who have mentioned him (and who has not?) witness with one voice."

Here our Lady is represented as rescuing a holy soul from intellectual error. This leads me to a further reflection. You seem, in one place in your volume, to object to the Antiphon, in which it is said of her, "All heresies thou hast destroyed alone." Surely the truth of it is verified in this age, as in former times, and especially by the doctrine concerning her, on which I have been dwelling. She is the great exemplar of prayer in a generation which emphatically denies the power of prayer *in toto*, which determines that fatal laws govern the universe, that there cannot be any direct communication between earth and heaven, that God cannot visit his own earth, and that man cannot influence God's providence. (*Difficulties of Anglicans*, pp. 68–76.)

Faith and Devotion

I CANNOT HELP hoping that your own reading of the Fathers will on the whole bear me out in the above account of their teaching concerning the Blessed Virgin. Anglicans seem to me simply to overlook the strength of the argument adducible from the works of those ancient doctors in our favor. They open the attack upon our medieval and modern writers, careless of leaving a host of primitive opponents in their rear. . . . Had you happened in your volume to introduce your notice of our teaching about the Blessed Virgin, with a notice of the teaching of the Fathers concerning her, which you follow, ordinary men would have considered that there was not much to choose between you and us. Though you appealed ever so much, in your defense, to the authority of the "undivided Church," they would have said that you, who had such high notions of the Blessed Mary, were one of the last men who had a right to accuse us of quasi-idolatry.

When they found you with the Fathers calling her Mother of God, Second Eve, and Mother of all Living, the Mother of Life, the Morning Star, the Mystical New Heaven, the Scepter of Orthodoxy, the All-undefiled Mother of Holiness, and the like, they would have deemed it a poor compensation for such language that you protested against her being called a co-redemptrix or a priestess. And if they were violent Protestants, they would not have read you with the relish and gratitude with which, as it is, they have perhaps accepted your testimony against us. Not that they would have been altogether fair in their view of you—on the contrary, I think there is a real difference between what you protest against and what with the Fathers you hold. But unread men of the world form a broad practical judgment of the things which come before them, and they would have felt in this case that they had the same right to be shocked at you as you have to be shocked at us—and further, which is the point to which I am coming, they would have said that, granting some of our modern writers go beyond the Fathers in this matter, still the line cannot be logically drawn between the teaching of the Fathers concerning the Blessed Virgin and our own. This view of the matter seems to me true and important, I do not think that the line can be satisfactorily drawn, and to this point I shall now direct my attention.

It is impossible, I say, in a doctrine like this, to draw the line cleanly between truth and error, right and wrong. This is ever the case in concrete matters, which have life. Life in this world is motion and involves a continual process of change. Living things grow into their perfection, into their decline, into their death. No rule of art will suffice to stop the operation of this natural law, whether in the material world or in the human mind. We can indeed encounter disorders, when they occur, by external antagonism and remedies; but we cannot eradicate the process itself, out of which they arise. Life has the same right to decay as it has to wax strong. This is specially the case with great ideas. You may stifle them; or you may refuse them elbow-room; or again, you may torment them with your continual meddling; or you may let them have free course and range, and be content, instead of anticipating their excesses, to expose and restrain those excesses after they have occurred. But you have only this alternative; and for myself, I prefer much wherever it is possible, to be first generous and then just, to grant full liberty of thought, and to call it to account when abused.

If what I have been saying be true of energetic ideas generally, much more is it the case in matters of religion. Religion acts on the affections; who is to hinder these, when once roused, from gathering in their strength and running wild? They are not gifted with any connatural principle within them, which renders them self-governing and self-adjusting. They hurry right on to their object, and often in their case it is, the more haste, the worse speed. Their object engrosses them, and they see nothing else. And of all passions love is the most unmanageable; nay more, I would not give much for that love which is never extravagant, which always observes the proprieties and can move about in perfect good taste, under all emergencies.

What mother, what husband or wife, what youth or maiden in love but says a thousand foolish things in the way of endearment, which the speaker would be sorry for strangers to hear; yet they are not on that account unwelcome to the parties to whom they are addressed. Sometimes by bad luck they are written down, sometimes they get into the newspapers; and what might be even graceful when it was fresh from the heart, and interpreted by the voice and the countenance, presents but a melancholy exhibition when served up cold for the public eye. So it is with devotional feelings. Burning thoughts and words are as open to criticism as they are beyond it. What is abstractedly extravagant, may in particular persons be becoming and beautiful, and only fall under blame when it is found in others who imitate them. When it is formalized into meditations and exercises, it is as repulsive as love letters in a police report.

Moreover, even holy minds adopt and become familiar with language which they would never have originated themselves, when it proceeds from a writer who has the same objects of devotion as they have. And, if they find a stranger ridicule or reprobate supplication or praise which has come to them so recommended, they feel it as keenly as if a direct insult were offered to those to whom that homage is addressed. In the next place, what has power to stir holy and refined souls is potent also with the multitude; and the religion of the multitude is ever vulgar and abnormal; it ever will be tinctured with fanaticism and superstition, while men are what they are.

A people's religion is ever a corrupt religion, in spite of the provisions of Holy Church. If she is to be Catholic, you must admit within her net fish of every kind, guests good and bad, vessels of gold, vessels of earth. You may beat religion out of men, if you will, and then their excesses will take a different direction; but if you make use of religion to improve them, they will make use of religion to corrupt it. And then you will have effected that compromise of which our countrymen report so unfavorably from abroad—a high grand faith and worship which compels their admiration, and puerile absurdities among the people which excite their contempt.

Nor is it any safeguard against these excesses in a religious system, that the religion is based upon reason and develops into a theology. Theology both uses logic and baffles it, and thus logic acts both for the protection and for the perversion of religion. Theology is occupied with supernatural matters, and is ever running into mysteries, which reason can neither explain nor adjust. Its lines of thought come to an abrupt termination, and to pursue them or to complete them is to plunge down the abyss. But logic blunders on, forcing its way, as it can, through thick darkness and ethereal mediums.

The Arians went ahead with logic for their directing principle, and so lost the truth. On the other hand, St. Augustine intimates that, if we attempt to find and tie together the ends of lines which run into infinity, we shall only succeed in contradicting ourselves when, in his "Treatise on the Holy Trinity," he is unable to find a logical reason for not speaking of three Gods as well as of One, and of one Person in the Godhead as well as of Three. I do not mean to say that logic cannot be used to set right its own error or that in the hands of an able disputant it may not trim the balance of truth. This was done at the Councils of Antioch and Nicaea, on occasion of the heresies of Paulus and Arius. But such a process is circuitous and elaborate and is conducted by means of minute subtleties which will give it the appearance of a game of skill in matters too grave and practical to deserve a mere scholastic treatment. Accordingly St. Augustine, in the treatise above mentioned, does no more than simply lay it down that the statements in question are heretical; that is, to say there are three Gods is Tritheism, and to say there is but one Person, Sabellianism. That is, good sense and a large view of truth are the correctives of his logic. And thus we have arrived at the final resolution of the matter, for good sense and a large view of truth are rare gifts; whereas all men are bound to be devout, and most men busy themselves in arguments and inferences.

Now let me apply what I have been saying to the teaching of the Church on the subject of the Blessed Virgin. I have to recur to a subject of so sacred a nature that, writing as I am for publication, I need the apology of my purpose for venturing to pursue it. I say then, when once we have mastered the idea that Mary bore, nursed, and handled the Eternal in the form of a child, what limit is conceivable to the rush and flood of thoughts which such a doctrine involves? What awe and surprise must attend upon the knowledge that a creature has been brought so close to the Divine Essence? It was the creation of a new idea and of a new sympathy, of a new faith and worship, when the holy apostles announced that God had become incarnate. Then a supreme love and devotion to him became possible, which seemed hopeless before that revelation. This was the first consequence of their preaching. But besides this, a second range of thoughts was opened upon mankind, unknown before, and unlike any other, as soon as it was understood that Incarnate God had a mother.

The second idea is perfectly distinct from the former and does not interfere with it. He is God made low, she is a woman made high. I scarcely like to use a familiar illustration on the subject of the Blessed Virgin's dignity among created beings, but it will serve to explain what I mean when I ask you to consider the difference of feeling with which we read the respective histories of Maria Theresa and the Maid of Orleans; or with which the middle and lower classes of a nation regard a first minister of the day who has come from an aristocratic house, and one who has risen from the ranks. May God's mercy keep me from the shadow of a thought, dimming the purity or blunting the keenness of that love of him which is our sole happiness and our sole salvation! But surely when he became man, he brought home to us his incommunicable attributes with a distinctiveness, which precludes the possibility of our lowering him merely by our exalting a creature. He alone has an entrance into our soul, reads our secret thoughts, speaks to our heart, applies to us spiritual pardon and strength. On him we solely depend. He alone is our inward life; he not only regenerates us, but (to use the words appropriated to a higher mystery) "*semper gignit,*" "He is ever renewing our new birth" and our heavenly sonship.

In this sense he may be called, as in nature, so in grace, our real Father. Mary is only our Mother by divine appointment, given us from the cross; her presence is above, not on earth; her office is external, not within us. Her name is not heard in the administration of the Sacraments. Her work is not one of ministration towards us; her power is indirect. It is her prayers that avail, and her prayers are effectual by the will of him who is our all in all. Nor need she hear us by any innate power, or any personal gift; but by his manifestation to her of the prayers which we make to her. When Moses was on the mount, the Almighty told him of the idolatry of his people at the foot of it, in order that he might intercede for them; and thus it is the Divine Presence which is the intermediating power by which we reach her and she reaches us.

Woe is me, if even by a breath I sully these ineffable truths! But still, without prejudice to them, there is, I say, another range of thought quite distinct from them, incommensurate with them, of which the Blessed Virgin is the center. If we placed our Lord in that center, we should only be dragging him from his throne and making him an Arian kind of a god; that is, no god at all. He who charges us with making Mary a divinity is thereby denying the divinity of Jesus. Such a man does not know what divinity is. Our Lord cannot pray for us, as a creature prays, as Mary prays; he cannot inspire those feelings which a creature inspires. To her belongs, as being a creature, a natural claim on our sympathy and familiarity, in that she is nothing else than our fellow. She is our pride—in the poet's words, "Our tainted nature's solitary boast."

We look at her without any fear, any remorse, any consciousness that she is able to read us, judge us, punish us. Our heart yearns towards that pure Virgin, that gentle Mother, and our congratulations follow her, as she rises from Nazareth and Ephesus, through the choir of angels, to her throne on high, so weak, yet so strong; so delicate, yet so glorious; so modest and yet so mighty. She has sketched for us her own portrait in the Magnificat. "He hath regarded the low estate of his handmaid; for, behold, from henceforth all generations shall call me blessed. He hath put down the mighty from their seat, and hath exalted the humble. He hath filled the hungry with good things, and the rich he hath sent empty away."

I recollect the strange emotion which took by surprise men and women, young and old, when, at the coronation of our present queen, they gazed on the figure of one so like a child, so small, so tender, so shrinking, who had been exalted to so great an inheritance and so vast a rule, who was in such a contrast in her own person to the solemn pageant which centered in her. Could it be otherwise with the spectators, if they had human affection? And did not the All-wise know the human heart when he took to himself a Mother? Did he not anticipate our emotion at the sight of such an exaltation in one so simple and so lowly?

If he had not meant her to exert that wonderful influence in his Church, which she has in the event exerted, I will use a bold word, he it is who has perverted us. If she is not to attract our homage, why did he make her solitary in her greatness amid his vast creation? If it be idolatry in us to let our affections respond to our faith, he would not have made her what she is, or he would not have told us that he had so made her; but, far from this, he has sent his prophet to announce to us, "A Virgin shall conceive and bear a Son, and they shall call his name Emmanuel." And we have the same warrant for hailing her as God's Mother, as we have for adoring him as God.

Christianity is eminently an objective religion. For the most part it tells of persons and facts in simple words, and leaves that announcement to produce its effect upon such hearts as are prepared to receive it. (This at least is its general character; and Butler recognizes it as such in his "Analogy," when speaking of the Second and Third Persons of the Holy Trinity. "The internal worship," he says, "to the Son and the Holy Ghost is no farther matter of pure revealed command than as the relations they stand in to us are matters of pure revelation; for the relations being known, the obligations to such internal worship are obligations of reason arising out of those relations themselves.")

It is in this way that the revealed doctrine of the Incarnation exerted a stronger and broader influence on Christians, as they more and more apprehended and mastered its meaning and its bearings. It is contained in the brief and simple declaration of St. John: "The Word was made Flesh"; but it required century after century to spread it out in its fullness and to imprint it energetically on the worship and practice of the Catholic people as well as on their faith. Athanasius was the first and the great teacher of it. He collected together the inspired notices scattered through

David, Isaiah, St. Paul, and St. John, and he engraved indelibly upon the imagination of the faithful, as had never been before, that man is God, and God is man, that in Mary they meet, and that in this sense Mary is the center of all things. He added nothing to what was known before, nothing to the popular and zealous faith that her Son was God. He has left behind him in his works no such definite passages about her as those of St. Irenaeus or St. Epiphanius; but he brought the circumstances of the Incarnation home to men's minds, by the multiform evolutions of his analysis, and thereby secured it to us forever from perversion.

Still, however, there was much to be done; we have no proof that Athanasius himself had any special devotion to the Blessed Virgin; but he laid the foundations on which that devotion was to rest, and thus noiselessly and without strife, as the first Temple was built in the Holy City, she grew up into her inheritance, and was "established in Zion and her power was in Jerusalem." (*Difficulties of Anglicans*, pp. 77–88.)

Mother of God

MERE PROTESTANTS have seldom any real perception of the doctrine of God and man in one Person. They speak in a dreamy, shadowy way of Christ's divinity; but, when their meaning is sifted, you will find them very slow to commit themselves to any statement sufficient to express the Catholic dogma. They will tell you at once that the subject is not to be inquired into, for that it is impossible to inquire into it at all without being technical and subtle. Then when they comment on the Gospels, they will speak of Christ, not simply and consistently as God, but as a being made up of God and man, partly one and partly the other, or between both, or as a man inhabited by a special divine presence.

Sometimes they even go on to deny that he was the Son of God in heaven, saying that he became the Son when he was conceived of the Holy Ghost. And they are shocked, and think it a mark both of reverence and good sense to be shocked, when they hear the Man spoken of simply and plainly as God. They cannot bear to have it except as a figure or mode of speaking, that God had a human body, or that God suffered. They think that the "atonement," and "sanctification through the Spirit," as they speak, is the sum and substance of the Gospel, and they are shy of any dogmatic expression which goes beyond them. Such, I believe, is the ordinary character of the Protestant notions among us on the divinity of Christ, whether among members of the Anglican communion, or dissenters from it, except for a small remnant of them.

Now, if you would witness against these unchristian opinions, if you would bring out, distinctly and beyond mistake and evasion, the simple idea of the Catholic Church that God is man, could you do it better than by laying down in St. John's words that "God became man"? And could you express this again more emphatically and unequivocally than by declaring that he was born a man, or that he had a mother? The world allows that God is man; the admission costs it little, for God is everywhere, and (as it may say) is everything; but it shrinks from confessing that God is the Son of Mary. It shrinks, for it is at once confronted with a severe fact, which violates and shatters its own unbelieving view of things. The revealed doctrine forthwith takes its true shape and receives an historical reality; and the Almighty is introduced into his own world at a certain time and in a definite way.

Dreams are broken and shadows depart; the divine truth is no longer a poetical expression, or a devotional exaggeration, or a mystical economy, or a mythical representation. "Sacrifice and offering" (the shadows of the Law) "thou wouldest not, but a body hast thou fitted to me." "That which was from the beginning, which we have heard, which we have seen with our eyes, which we have diligently looked upon, and our hands have handled," "That which we have seen and have heard, declare we unto you"; such is the record of the apostle, in opposition to those "spirits" which denied that "Jesus Christ had appeared in the flesh," and which "dissolved" him by denying either his human nature or his divine.

And the confession that Mary is Deipara, or the Mother of God, is that safeguard wherewith we seal up and secure the doctrine of the apostle from all evasion, and that test whereby we detect all the pretenses of those bad spirits of "antichrist which have gone out into the world." It declares that he is God; it implies that he is man; it suggests to us that he is God still, though he has become man, and that he is true man though he is God. By wit-

nessing to the process of the union, it secures the reality of the two
subjects of the union, of the divinity, and of the manhood. If Mary
is the Mother of God, Christ is understood to be Emmanuel, God
with us.

And hence it was that, when time went on, and the bad spirits and false prophets grew stronger and bolder and found a way
into the Catholic body itself, then the Church, guided by God,
could find no more effectual and sure way of expelling them than
that of using this word Deipara against them. On the other hand,
when they came up again from the realms of darkness, and plot-
ted the utter overthrow of Christian faith in the sixteenth century, then they could find no more certain expedient for their
hateful purpose than that of reviling and blaspheming the prerogatives of Mary. For they knew full sure that, if they could once
get the world to dishonor the Mother, the dishonor of the Son
would follow close.

The Church and Satan agreed together in this, that Son and
Mother went together; and the experience of three centuries has
confirmed their testimony; for Catholics who have honored the
Mother still worship the Son, while Protestants, who now have
ceased to confess the Son, began then by scoffing at the Mother.
(*Discourses to Mixed Congregations*, pp. 345–48.)

Mother Most Pure

MARY HAS been made more glorious in her person than in her office; her purity is a higher gift than her relationship to God. This is what is implied in Christ's answer to the woman in the crowd who cried out, when he was preaching, "Blessed is the womb that bore thee, and the breasts which thou hast sucked." He replied by pointing out to his disciples a higher blessedness; "Yea, rather blessed," he said, "are they who hear the word of God and keep it. . ."

Protestants take these words in disparagement of our Lady's greatness, but they really tell the other way. For consider them; he lays down a principle that it is more blessed to keep his commandments than to be his Mother, but who even of Protestants will say that she did not keep his commandments? She kept them surely, and our Lord does but say that such obedience was in a higher line of privilege than her being his Mother. She was more blessed in her detachment from creatures, in her devotion to God, in her virginal purity, in her fullness of grace, than in her maternity. This is the constant teaching of the holy Fathers: "More blessed was Mary," says St. Augustine, "in receiving Christ's faith, than in conceiving Christ's flesh." And St. Chrysostom declares that she would not have been blessed, though she had borne him in the body, had she not heard the word of God and kept it.

This of course is an impossible case; for she was made holy that she might be made his Mother, and the two blessednesses cannot be divided. She who was chosen to supply flesh and blood to the Eternal Word was first filled with grace in soul and body. Still, she had a double blessedness, of office and of qualification for it, and the latter was the greater. And it is on this account that the angel calls her blessed. "Full of grace," he says, "blessed among women"; and St. Elizabeth also, when she cries out, "Blessed thou that has believed." Nay, she herself bears a like testimony, when the Angel announced to her the favor which was coming on her.

Though all Jewish women in each successive age had been hoping to be mother of the Christ, so that marriage was honorable among them, celibacy a reproach, she alone had put aside the desire and the thought of so great a dignity. She alone, who was to bear the Christ, all but refused to bear him. He stooped to her, she turned from him. And why?—because she had been inspired, the first of womankind, to dedicate her virginity to God, and she did not welcome a privilege which seemed to involve a forfeiture of her vow. "How shall this be," she asked, "seeing I am separate from man?" Nor, till the angel told her that the conception would be miraculous and from the Holy Ghost, did she put aside her "trouble" of mind, recognize him securely as God's messenger, and bow her head in awe and thankfulness to God's condescension.

Mary then is a specimen, and more than a specimen, in the purity of her soul and body, of what man was before his fall and what he would have been, had he risen to his full perfection. It would have been hard, it would have been a victory for the Evil One, if the whole race had passed away, without one instance occurring to show what the Creator had intended it to be in its original state. Adam, you know, was created in the image and after the likeness of God. His frail and imperfect nature, stamped with a divine seal, was supported and exalted by an indwelling of divine grace. Impetuous passion did not exist in him, except as a latent element and a possible evil; ignorance was dissipated by the clear light of the Spirit; and reason, sovereign over every motion of his soul, was simply subjected to the will of God. Nay, even his body was preserved from every wayward appetite and affection and was promised immortality instead of dissolution.

Thus he was in a supernatural state; and, had he not sinned, he would have advanced in merit and grace and in God's favor year after year, till he passed from Paradise to heaven. But he fell; and his descendants were born in his likeness; and the world grew worse instead of better, and judgment after judgment cut off generations of sinners in vain, and improvement was hopeless, "because man was flesh," and "the thoughts of his heart were bent upon evil at all times."

But a remedy had been determined in heaven; a Redeemer was at hand; God was about to do a great work, and he purposed to do it suitably; "where sin abounded, grace was to abound more." Kings of the earth, when they have sons born to them, forthwith scatter some large bounty, or raise some high memorial; they honor the day, or the place, or the heralds of the auspicious event, with some corresponding mark of favor; nor did the coming of Emmanuel innovate on the world's established custom. It was a season of grace and prodigy, and these were to be exhibited in a special manner in the person of his Mother. The course of ages was to be reversed; the tradition of evil was to be broken; a gate of light was to be opened amid the darkness, for the coming of the Just; a Virgin conceived and bore him. It was fitting, for his honor and glory, that she who was the instrument of his bodily presence, should first be a miracle of his grace; it was fitting that she should triumph, where Eve had failed, and should "bruise the serpent's head" by the spotlessness of her sanctity. In some respects, indeed, the curse was not reversed; Mary came into a fallen world and resigned herself to its laws. She, as also the Son she bore, was exposed to pain of soul and body. She was subjected to death, but she was not put under the power of sin.

As grace was infused into Adam from the first moment of his creation, so that he never had experience of his natural poverty till sin reduced him to it; so was grace given from the first in still ampler measure to Mary, and she never incurred, in fact, Adam's deprivation. She began where others end, whether in knowledge or in love. She was from the first clothed in sanctity, sealed for perseverance, luminous and glorious in God's sight, and incessantly employed in meritorious acts, which continued till her last breath. Hers was emphatically "the path of the just, which, as the shining light, goeth forward and increaseth even to the perfect day." And sinlessness in thought, word, and deed, in small things as well as great, in venial matter as well as grievous, is surely but the natural and obvious sequel of such a beginning. If Adam might have kept himself from sin in his first state, much more shall we expect immaculate perfection in Mary. (*Discourses to Mixed Congregations,* pp. 350–54.)

Refuge of Sinners

SUCH IS her prerogative of sinless perfection, and it is, as her maternity, for the sake of Emmanuel. Hence she answered the angel's salutation, *"Gratia plena,"* with the humble acknowledgment, *"Ecce ancilla Domini"* (Behold the handmaid of the Lord). And like to this is her third prerogative, which follows both from her maternity and from her purity, and which I will mention as completing the enumeration of her glories. I mean her intercessory power. For if "God heareth not sinners, but if a man be a worshipper of him and do his will, him he heareth"; if "the continual prayer of a just man availeth much"; if faithful Abraham was required to pray for Abimelech, "for he was a prophet"; if patient Job was to "pray for his friends," for he had "spoken right things before God"; if meek Moses, by lifting up his hands, turned the battle in favor of Israel, against Amalec; why should we wonder at hearing that Mary, the only spotless child of Adam's seed, has a transcendent influence with the God of grace?

And if the Gentiles at Jerusalem sought Philip, because he was an apostle, when they desired access to Jesus, and Philip spoke to Andrew, as still more closely in our Lord's confidence, and then both came to him, is it strange that the Mother should have power with the Son, distinct in kind from that of the purest angel and the most triumphant saint?

If we have faith to admit the Incarnation itself, we must admit it in its fullness; why then should we be surprised by the gracious appointments which arise out of it, or are necessary to it, or are included in it? If the Creator comes on earth in the form of a servant and a creature, why may not his Mother on the other hand rise to be the Queen of Heaven, and be clothed with the sun, and have the moon under her feet? (*Discourses to Mixed Congregations,* pp. 354–55.)

Conceived without Original Sin

W E SHOULD be prepared . . . to believe that the Mother of
God is full of grace and glory, from the very fitness of such
a dispensation, even though we had not been taught it. And this
fitness will appear still more clear and certain when we contemplate the subject more steadily.

Consider, then, that it has been the ordinary rule of God's
dealings with us that personal sanctity should be the attendant
upon high spiritual dignity of place or work. The angels who, as
the word imports, are God's messengers are also perfect in holiness; "without sanctity no one shall see God." No defiled thing can
enter the courts of heaven; and the higher its inhabitants are advanced in their ministry about the throne, the holier are they and
the more absorbed in their contemplation of that Holiness upon
which they wait.

The Seraphim, who immediately surround the Divine Glory,
cry day and night, "Holy, Holy, Holy, Lord God of Hosts." So is it
also on earth; the prophets have ordinarily not only gifts, but
graces. They are not only inspired to know and to teach God's will
but inwardly converted to obey it. For surely those only can
preach the truth duly who feel it personally. Those only transmit
it fully from God to man who have in the transmission made it
their own.

I do not say that there are no exceptions to this rule, but they
admit of an easy explanation. I do not say that it never pleases
Almighty God to convey any intimation of his will through bad

men; of course, for all things can be made to serve him. By all, even the wicked, he accomplishes his purposes, and by the wicked he is glorified.

Our Lord's death was brought about by his enemies, who did his will while they thought they were gratifying their own. Caiaphas, who contrived and effected it, was made use of to predict it. Balaam prophesied good of God's people in an earlier age, by a divine compulsion, when he wished to prophesy evil. This is true; but in such cases Divine Mercy is plainly overruling the evil and manifesting his power, without recognizing or sanctioning the instrument. And again, it is true, as he tells us himself, that in the last day "Many shall say, Lord, Lord, have we not prophesied in thy name, and in thy name cast out devils, and done many miracles?" and that he shall answer, "I never knew you." This, I say, is undeniable; it is undeniable first, that those who have prophesied in God's name may afterwards fall from God and lose their souls.

Let a man be ever so holy now, he may fall away; and, as present grace is no pledge of perseverance, much less are present gifts; but how does this show that gifts and graces do not commonly go together? Again, it is undeniable that those who have had miraculous gifts may nevertheless have never been in God's favor, not even when they exercised them, as I will explain presently. But I am now speaking, not of having gifts, but of being prophets. To be a prophet is something much more personal than to possess gifts. It is a sacred office, it implies a mission, and is the high distinction, not of the enemies of God, but of his friends. Such is the Scripture rule.

Who was the first prophet and preacher of justice? Enoch, who walked "by faith," and "pleased God," and was taken from a rebellious world. Who was the second? "Noah," who "condemned the world, and was made heir of the justice which is through faith." Who was the next great prophet? Moses, the lawgiver of the chosen people, who was the "meekest of all men who dwell on the

earth." Samuel comes next, who served the Lord from his infancy
in the Temple; and then David, who, if he fell into sin, repented,
and was "a man after God's heart." And in like manner Job, Elias,
Isaiah, Jeremiah, Daniel, and, above them all, St. John the Baptist,
and then again St. Peter, St. Paul, St. John, and the rest, are all es-
pecial instances of heroic virtue, and patterns to their brethren.
Judas is the exception, but this was by a particular dispensation to
enhance our Lord's humiliation and suffering.

Nature itself witnesses to this connection between sanctity
and truth. It anticipates that the fountain from which pure doctrine comes should itself be pure; that the seat of divine teaching,
and the oracle of faith, should be the abode of angels; that the
consecrated home, in which the word of God is elaborated, and
whence it issues forth for the salvation of the many, should be
holy as that word is holy. Here you see the difference of the
office of a prophet and a mere gift, such as that of miracles. Miracles are the simple and direct work of God; the worker of them
is but an instrument or organ. And in consequence he need not
be holy, because he has not, strictly speaking, a share in the work.
So again the power of administering the Sacraments, which also
is supernatural and miraculous, does not imply personal holiness;
nor is there anything surprising in God's giving to a bad man this
gift, or the gift of miracles, any more than in his giving him any
natural talent or gift, strength or agility of frame, eloquence, or
medical skill.

It is otherwise with the office of preaching and prophesying,
and to this I have been referring; for the truth first goes into the
minds of the speakers, and is apprehended and fashioned there,
and then comes out from them as, in one sense, its source and its
parent. The divine word is begotten in them, and the offspring has
their features and tells of them. They are not like "the dumb ani-
mal, speaking with man's voice," on which Balaam rode, a mere
instrument of God's word, but they have "received an unction

from the Holy One, and they know all things," and "where the Spirit of the Lord is, there is liberty"; and while they deliver what they have received, they enforce what they feel and know. "We have known and believed," says St. John, "the charity which God hath to us."

So has it been all through the history of the Church, Moses does not write as David; nor Isaiah as Jeremiah; nor St. John as St. Paul. And so of the great doctors of the Church, St. Athanasius, St. Augustine, St. Ambrose, St. Leo, St. Thomas, each has his own manner, each speaks his own words, though he speaks the while the words of God. They speak from themselves, they speak in their own persons, they speak from the heart, from their own experience, with their own arguments, with their own deductions, with their own modes of expression.

Now can you fancy such hearts, such feelings to be unholy? How could it be so, without defiling, and thereby nullifying, the word of God? If one drop of corruption makes the purest water worthless, as the slightest savor of bitterness spoils the most delicate viands, how can it be that the word of truth and holiness can proceed profitably from impure lips and an earthly heart? No, as is the tree, so is the fruit. "Beware of false prophets," says our Lord; and then he adds, "from their fruits ye shall know them. Do men gather grapes of thorns, or figs of thistles?" Is it not so, my brethren?

Which of you would go to ask counsel of another, however learned, however gifted, however aged, if you thought him unholy? Nay, though you feel and are sure, as far as absolution goes, that a bad priest could give it as validly as a holy priest, yet for advice, for comfort, for instruction, you would not go to one whom you did not respect. "Out of the abundance of the heart, the mouth speaketh"; "a good man out of the good treasure of his heart bringeth good, and an evil man out of the evil treasure bringeth forth evil."

So then is it in the case of the soul; and so is it with the body also. As the offspring of holiness is holy in the instance of spiritual births, so is it in the instance of physical. The child is like the parent. Mary was no mere instrument in God's dispensation. The Word of God did not merely come to her and go from her. He did not merely pass through her, as he may pass through us in Holy Communion. It was no heavenly body which the Eternal Son assumed, fashioned by the angels, and brought down to this lower world. No, he imbibed, he sucked up her blood and her substance into his Divine Person. He became man of her, and received her lineaments and her features as the appearance and character under which he should manifest himself to the world. He was known doubtless, by his likeness to her, to be her Son.

Thus his Mother is the first of prophets, for of her came the Word bodily. She is the sole oracle of truth, for the Way, the Truth, and the Life vouchsafed to be her Son. She is the one mold of Divine Wisdom, and in that mold it was indelibly cast. Surely then, if "the first fruit be holy, the mass also is holy; and if the root be holy, so are the branches." It was natural, it was fitting, that so it should be. It was congruous that, whatever the Omnipotent could work in the person of the finite, should be wrought in her.

I say, if the prophets must be holy, "to whom the word of God comes," what shall we say of her, who was so specially favored, that the true and substantial Word, and not his shadow or his voice, was not merely made in her, but born of her?—who was not merely the organ of God's message but the origin of his human existence, the living fountain from which he drew his most precious blood and the material of his most holy flesh? Was it not fitting, beseemed it not, that the Eternal Father should prepare her for this ministration by some preeminent sanctification? Do not earthly parents act thus by their children? Do they put them out to strangers? Do they commit them to any chance person to suckle them? Shall even careless parents show a certain tenderness and solicitude in this matter, and shall not God himself show it, when he commits his Eternal Word to the custody of man?

It was to be expected then that, if the Son was God, the Mother should be as worthy of him, as creature can be worthy of Creator; that grace should have in her its "perfect work"; that, if she bore the Eternal Wisdom, she should be that created wisdom in whom "is all the grace of the Way and the Truth"; that if she was the Mother of "fair love, and fear, and knowledge, and holy hope," "she should give an odor like cinnamon and balm, and sweetness like to choice myrrh." Can we set bounds to the holiness of her who was the Mother of the Holiest?

Such, then, is the truth ever cherished in the deep heart of the Church and witnessed by the keen apprehension of her children, that no limits but those proper to a creature can be assigned to the sanctity of Mary. Did Abraham believe that a son should be born to him of his aged wife?—then Mary's faith was greater when she accepted Gabriel's message. Did Judith consecrate her widowhood to God to the surprise of her people?—much more did Mary, from her first youth, devote her virginity. Did Samuel, when a child, inhabit the Temple, secluded from the world? Mary, too, was by her parents lodged in the same holy precincts, at the age when children begin to choose between good and evil. Was Solomon on his birth called "dear to the Lord"? And shall not the destined Mother of God be dear to him, from the moment she was born?

But further still: St. John the Baptist was sanctified by the Spirit before his birth; shall Mary be only equal to him? Is it not fitting that her privilege should surpass his? Is it a cause of wonder, if grace, which anticipated his birth by three months, should in her case run up to the very first moment of her being, outstrip the imputation of sin, and be beforehand with the usurpation of Satan?

Mary must surpass all the saints; the very fact that certain privileges are known to have been theirs, proves to us at once, from the necessity of the case, that she had the same and higher. Her conception then was immaculate, in order that she might surpass all saints in the date as well as the fullness of her sanctification. (*Discourses to Mixed Congregations,* pp. 364–70.)

The Assumption of Mary

IT WAS surely fitting, it was becoming, that she should be taken
up into heaven and not lie in the grave till Christ's second coming, she who had passed such a life of sanctify and of miracles. All
the works of God are in a beautiful harmony; they are carried on
to the end as they begin. This is the difficulty which men of the
world find in believing miracles at all. They think these break the
order and consistency of God's visible world, not knowing that
they do but subserve a higher order of things, and introduce a supernatural perfection.

But at least, when one miracle is wrought, it may be expected
to draw others after it for the completion of what is begun. Miracles must be wrought for some great end; and if the course of
things fell back again into a natural order before its termination,
how could we but feel a disappointment? And if we were told that
this certainly was to be, how could we but judge the information
improbable and difficult to believe?

Now this applies to the history of our Lady. I say, it would be
a greater miracle, if, her life being what it was, her death were to
be like that of other men and women, than if it were such as to
correspond to her life. Who can conceive that God should so repay
the debt, which he condescended to owe to his Mother, for the elements of his human body, as to allow the flesh and blood from
which it was taken to molder in the grave? Do the sons of men
thus deal with their mothers? Do they not nourish and sustain
them in their feebleness, and keep them in life while they are able?
Or who can conceive that that virginal frame, which never sinned,

was to undergo the death of a sinner? Why should she share the curse of Adam, who had no share in his fall?

"Dust thou art, and into dust thou shalt return," was the sentence upon sin. She then, who was not a sinner, fitly never saw corruption. She died then because even our Lord and Savior died. She died, as she suffered, because she was in this world, because she was in a state of things in which suffering and death are the rule. She lived under their external sway; and, as she obeyed Caesar by coming for enrollment to Bethlehem, so did she, when God willed it, yield to the tyranny of death, and was dissolved into soul and body, as well as others. But though she died as well as others, she died not as others die. For, through the merits of her Son, by whom she was what she was—by the grace of Christ which in her had anticipated sin, which had filled her with light, which had purified her flesh from all defilement—she had been saved from disease and malady and all that weakens and decays the bodily frame. Original sin had not been found in her, by the wear of her senses, and the waste of her frame, and the decrepitude of years, propagating death.

She died, but her death was a mere fact, not an effect; and, when it was over, it ceased to be. She died that she might live; she died as a matter of form or (as I may call it) a ceremony, in order to fulfill what is called the debt of nature—not primarily for herself or because of sin, but to submit herself to her condition, to glorify God, to do what her Son did. She did not however die as her Son and Savior, with any suffering for any special end; not with a martyr's death, for her martyrdom had been in living; not as an atonement, for man could not make it, and One had made it and made it for all; but in order to finish her course, and to receive her crown.

And therefore she died in private. It became him who died for the world, to die in the world's sight. It became the Great Sacrifice to be lifted up on high, as a light that could not be hid. But she, the lily of Eden, who had always dwelt out of the sight of man, fittingly did she die in the garden's shade, and amid the sweet flowers in which she had lived. Her departure made no noise in the world.

The Church went about her common duties, preaching, conversing, suffering. There were persecutions, there was fleeing from place to place, there were martyrs, there were triumphs. At length the rumor spread abroad that the Mother of God was no longer upon earth. Pilgrims went to and fro; they sought for her relics, but they found them not. Did she die at Ephesus? Or did she die at Jerusalem? Reports varied, but her tomb could not be pointed out. If it was found, it was open, and instead of her pure and fragrant body, there was a growth of lilies from the earth which she had touched. So, inquirers went home marvelling, and waiting for further light.

And then it was said how that when her dissolution was at hand, and her soul was to pass in triumph before the judgment seat of her Son, the apostles were suddenly gathered together in one place, in the Holy City itself, to bear part in the joyful ceremonial; how that they buried her with fitting rites; how that the third day, when they came to the tomb, they found it empty, and angelic choirs with their glad voices were heard singing day and night the glories of their risen queen. But, however we feel towards the details of this history (nor is there anything in it which will be unwelcome or difficult to piety), so much cannot be doubted, from the consent of the whole Catholic world and the revelations made to holy souls, that as is befitting, she is, soul and body, with her Son and God in heaven, and that we are enabled to celebrate not only her death, but her Assumption. (*Discourses to Mixed Congregations,* pp. 370–74.)

Growth of the Cultus of Mary

ONE WORD more, and I have done; I have shown you how full of meaning are the truths themselves which the Church teaches concerning the Most Blessed Virgin, and now consider how full of meaning also has been the Church's dispensation of them.

You will find, then, in this respect, as in Mary's prerogatives themselves, there is the same careful reference to the glory of him who gave them to her. You know, when first he went out to preach, she kept apart from him; she interfered not with his work. Even when he was gone up on high, she, a woman, went not out to preach or teach, she seated not herself in the apostolic chair, she took no part in the priest's office. She did but humbly seek her Son in the daily Mass of those who, though her ministers in heaven, were her superiors in the Church on earth. Nor, when she and they had left this lower scene, and she was a queen upon her Son's right hand, not even then did she ask of him to publish her name unto the ends of the world, or to hold her up to the world's gaze, but she remained waiting for the time when her own glory should be necessary for his.

He indeed had been from the very first proclaimed by Holy Church and enthroned in his temple, for he was God. Ill had it be-seemed the living Oracle of Truth to have withheld from the faithful the very object of their adoration, but it was otherwise with Mary. It became her, as a creature, a mother, and a woman, to stand aside and make way for the Creator, to minister to her Son, and to win her way into the world's homage by sweet and gracious persuasion. So when his name was dishonored, then it was that she did him service. When Emmanuel was denied, then the Mother of God (as it were) came forward. When heretics said that God was not incarnate, then was the time for her own honors. And then, when as much as this had been accomplished, she had done with strife; she fought not for herself. No fierce controversy, no persecuted confessors, no heresiarch, no anathema marks the history of her manifestation.

As she had increased day by day in grace and merit, while the world knew not of it, so has she raised herself aloft silently, and has grown into her place in the Church by a tranquil influence and a natural process. It was as some fair tree, stretching forth her fruitful branches and her fragrant leaves, and overshadowing the territory of the saints. And thus the antiphon speaks of her: "Let thy dwelling be in Jacob, and shine inheritance in Israel, and strike thy roots in my elect." Again, "And so in Zion was I established, and in the Holy City I likewise rested, and Jerusalem was my power. And I took root in an honorable people, and in the glorious company of the saints was I detained. I was exalted like a cedar in Lebanon, and as a cypress in Mount Zion; I have stretched out my branches as the terebinth, and my branches are of honor and of grace."

Thus was she reared without hands, and gained a modest victory, and exerts a gentle sway, which she has not claimed. When dispute arose about her among her children, she hushed it. When objections were urged against her, she waived her claims and waited. Till now, in this very day, should God so will, she will win at length her most radiant crown, and without opposing voice, and amid the jubilation of the whole Church, she will be hailed as immaculate in her conception.

Such art thou, Holy Mother, in the Creed and in the worship of the Church, the defense of many truths, the grace and smiling

light of every devotion. In thee, O Mary, is fulfilled, as we can bear
it, an original purpose of the Most High. He once had meant to
come on earth in heavenly glory, but we sinned; and then he could
not safely visit us, except with shrouded radiance and a bedimmed
majesty, for he was God. So he came himself in weakness, not in
power; and he sent thee a creature in his stead, with a creature's
comeliness and lustre suited to our state. And now thy very face
and form, dear Mother, speak to us of the Eternal; not like earthly
beauty, dangerous to look upon, but like the morning star, which
is thy emblem, bright and musical, breathing purity, telling of
heaven, and infusing peace. O harbinger of day! O hope of the pilgrim! Lead us still as thou hast led; in the dark night, across the
bleak wilderness, guide us on to our Lord Jesus, guide us home.

> Maria, mater gratiae,
> Dulcis parens clementiae,
> Tu nos ab hoste protege,
> Et mortis hora suscipe.

> [Mary, mother of grace,
> Gentle, compassionate parent,
> Protect us from the enemy,
> And receive us at the hour of death.]

(*Discourses to Mixed Congregations,* pp. 357–60.)

Part II

May, the Month of Promise and of Joy

WHY IS MAY chosen as the month in which we exercise a special devotion to the Blessed Virgin?

The first reason is because it is the time when the earth bursts forth into its fresh foliage and its green grass after the stern frost and snow of winter, and the raw atmosphere and the wild wind and rain of the early spring. It is because the blossoms are upon the trees and the flowers are in the gardens. It is because the days have got long, and the sun rises early and sets late. For such gladness and joyousness of external nature is a fit attendant on our devotion to her who is the Mystical Rose and the House of Gold.

A man may say, "True; but in this climate we have sometimes a bleak, inclement May." This cannot be denied; but still, so much is true that at least it is the month of promise and of hope. Even though the weather happen to be bad, it is the month that begins and heralds in the summer. We know, for all that may be unpleasant in it, that fine weather is coming sooner or later. "Brightness and beautifulness shall," in the prophet's words, "appear at the end, and shall not lie: if it make delay, wait for it, for it shall surely come, and shall not be slack."

May then is the month, if not of fulfillment, at least of promise; and is not this the very aspect in which we most suitably regard the Blessed Virgin, Holy Mary, to whom this month is dedicated?

The prophet says, "There shall come forth a rod out of the root of Jesse, and a flower shall rise out of his root." Who is the flower but our Blessed Lord? Who is the rod, or beautiful stalk, or

69

stem, or plant out of which the flower grows, but Mary, Mother of our Lord, Mary, Mother of God?

It was prophesied that God should come upon earth. When the time was now full, how was it announced? It was announced by the angel coming to Mary. "Hail, full of grace," said Gabriel, "the Lord is with thee; blessed art thou among women." She then was the sure promise of the coming Savior, and therefore May is by a special title her month.

Why is May called the month of Mary and especially dedicated to her? Among other reasons there is this: that of the Church's year, the ecclesiastical year, it is at once the most sacred and the most festive and joyous portion. Who would wish February, March, or April, to be the month of Mary, considering that it is the time of Lent and penance? Who again would choose December, the Advent season—a time of hope, indeed, because Christmas is coming, but a time of fasting too? Christmas itself does not last for a month; and January has indeed the joyful Epiphany, with its Sundays in succession; but these in most years are cut short by the urgent coming of Septuagesima.

May on the contrary belongs to the Easter season, which lasts fifty days, and in that season the whole of May commonly falls, and the first half always. The great feast of the Ascension of our Lord into heaven is always in May, except once or twice in forty years. Pentecost, called also Whit-Sunday, the feast of the Holy Ghost, is commonly in May, and the feasts of the Holy Trinity and Corpus Christi are in May not unfrequently. May, therefore, is the time in which there are such frequent alleluias, because Christ has risen from the grave, Christ has ascended on high, and God the Holy Ghost has come down to take his place.

Here then we have a reason why May is dedicated to the Blessed Mary. She is the first of creatures, the most acceptable child of God, the dearest and nearest to him. It is fitting then that this month should be hers, in which we especially glory and rejoice in his great providence to us, in our redemption and sanctification in God the Father, God the Son, and God the Holy Ghost.

But Mary is not only the acceptable handmaid of the Lord. She is also Mother of his Son and the Queen of all Saints, and in this month the Church has placed the feasts of some of the greatest of them, as if to bear her company.

First, however, there is the Feast of the Holy Cross, on the third of May, when we venerate that Precious Blood in which the cross was bedewed at the time of our Lord's Passion. The archangel St. Michael and three apostles have feast-days in this month: St. John the beloved disciple, St. Philip, and St. James; seven popes, two of them especially famous, St. Gregory VII and St. Pius V; also two of the greatest doctors, St. Athanasius and St. Gregory Nazianzen; two holy virgins especially favored by God, St. Catherine of Siena (as her feast is kept in England) and St. Mary Magdalen of Pazzi; and one holy woman most memorable in the annals of the Church, St. Monica, the mother of St. Augustine. And above all, and nearest to us in this church, our own holy patron and father, St. Philip [Neri], occupies, with his novena and octave, fifteen out of the whole thirty-one days of the month. These are some of the choicest fruits of God's manifold grace, and they form the court of their glorious queen. (*Meditations and Devotions* [Longmans, Green: London, 1953], pp. 1–5.)

Virgin Most Pure

B Y THE Immaculate Conception of the Blessed Virgin is meant the great revealed truth that she was conceived in the womb of her mother, St. Anne, without original sin.

Since the fall of Adam all mankind, his descendants, are conceived and born in sin. "Behold," says the inspired writer in the Psalm Miserere: "Behold, I was conceived in iniquity, and in sin did my mother conceive me." That sin which belongs to every one of us, and is ours from the first moment of our existence, is the sin of unbelief and disobedience by which Adam lost Paradise. We, as the children of Adam, are heirs to the consequences of his sin, and have forfeited in him that spiritual robe of grace and holiness which he had given him by his Creator at the time that he was made. In this state of forfeiture and disinheritance we are all of us conceived and born; and the ordinary way by which we are taken out of it is the Sacrament of Baptism.

But Mary never was in this state; she was by the eternal decree of God exempted from it. From eternity, God, the Father, Son, and Holy Ghost decreed to create the race of man and, foreseeing the fall of Adam, decreed to redeem the whole race by the Son's taking flesh and suffering on the cross.

In that same incomprehensible, eternal instant, in which the Son of God was born of the Father, was also the decree passed of man's redemption through him. He who was born from eternity was born by an eternal decree to save us in time and to redeem the whole race; and Mary's redemption was determined in that special manner which we call the Immaculate Conception.

It was decreed, not that she should be cleansed from sin, but that she should, from the first moment of her being, be preserved from sin; so that the Evil One never had any part in her. Therefore she was a child of Adam and Eve as if they had never fallen; she did not share with them their sin; she inherited the gifts and graces (and more than those) which Adam and Eve possessed in Paradise. This is her prerogative and the foundation of all those salutary truths which are revealed to us concerning her. Let us say then with all holy souls, Virgin most pure, conceived without original sin, Mary, pray for us. (*Meditations and Devotions*, pp. 6–7.)

Virgin Most Renowned

M ARY IS the *Virgo Praedicanda* [Virgin Most Renowned], that is, the Virgin who is to be proclaimed, to be heralded; literally, to be preached.

We are accustomed to preach abroad that which is wonderful, strange, rare, novel, important. Thus, when our Lord was coming, St. John the Baptist preached him; then, the apostles went into the wide world and preached Christ.

What is the highest, the rarest, the choicest prerogative of Mary? It is that she was without sin. When a woman in the crowd cried out to our Lord, "Blessed is the womb that bore thee!" he answered, "More blessed are they who hear the word of God and keep it."

Those words were fulfilled in Mary. She was filled with grace in order to be the Mother of God. But it was a higher gift than her maternity to be thus sanctified and thus pure. Our Lord indeed would not have become her Son unless he had first sanctified her; but still, the greater blessedness was to have that perfect sanctification. This then is why she is the Virgin Most Renowned. She is deserving to be preached abroad because she never committed any sin, even the least; because sin had no part in her; because, through the fullness of God's grace, she never thought a thought, or spoke a word or did an action, which was displeasing, which was not most pleasing, to Almighty God; because in her was displayed the greatest triumph over the enemy of souls.

Wherefore, when all seemed lost, in order to show what he could do for us all by dying for us; in order to show what human nature, his work, was capable of becoming; to show how utterly he could bring to naught the utmost efforts, the most concentrated malice of the foe, and reverse all the consequences of the fall, our Lord began, even before his coming, to do his most wonderful act of redemption, in the person of her who was to be his Mother. By the merit of that blood which was to be shed, he interposed to hinder her incurring the sin of Adam, before he had made on the cross atonement for it. And therefore it is that we preach her who is the subject of this wonderful grace.

But she was the Virgin Most Renowned for another reason. When, why, what things do we preach? We preach what is not known, that it may become known. And hence the apostles are said in Scripture to "preach Christ." To whom? To those who knew him not—to the heathen world. Not to those who knew him, but to those who did not know him. Preaching is a gradual work: first one lesson, then another. Thus were the heathen brought into the Church *gradually.*

And in like manner, the preaching of Mary to the children of the Church, and the devotion paid to her by them, has *grown,* grown gradually, with successive ages. Not so much was preached about her in early times as in later. First she was preached as the Virgin of Virgins—then as the Mother of God—then as glorious in her Assumption—then as the advocate of sinners—then as Immaculate in her Conception. And this last has been the special preaching of the present century; and thus, that which was earliest in her own history is the latest in the Church's recognition of her. * (*Meditations and Devotions,* pp. 8–10.)

---

*Newman was, of course, writing long before Pope Pius XII's official declaration of the Assumption as a dogma of the faith in 1950. He is referring to it, therefore, as an accepted doctrine taught by the ordinary magisterium of the Church.—Ed.

Mother Most Admirable

W HEN MARY, the Virgin Most Renowned, the Virgin who is to be proclaimed aloud, is called by the title of Most Admirable, it is thereby suggested to us what the effect is of the preaching of her as Immaculate in her Conception. The Holy Church proclaims, preaches her, as conceived without original sin; and those who hear, the children of Holy Church, wonder, marvel, are astonished and overcome by the preaching. It is so great a prerogative.

Even created excellence is fearful to think of when it is so high as Mary's. As to the great Creator, when Moses desired to see his glory, he himself says about himself, "Thou canst not see my face, for man shall not see me and live"; and St. Paul says, "Our God is a consuming fire." And when St. John, holy as he was, saw only the *human nature* of our Lord, as he is in heaven, "he fell at his feet as dead." And so as regards the appearance of angels. The holy Daniel, when St. Gabriel appeared to him, "fainted away, and lay in a consternation, with his face close to the ground." When this great archangel came to Zechariah, the father of St. John the Baptist, he too "was troubled, and fear fell upon him." But it was otherwise with Mary when the same St. Gabriel came to her. She was overcome indeed, and troubled at his *words,* because, humble as she was in her own opinion of herself, he addressed her as "full of grace" and "blessed among women"; but she was able to bear the sight of him.

Hence we learn two things: first, how great a holiness was Mary's, seeing she could endure the presence of an angel whose brightness smote the holy prophet Daniel even to fainting and almost to death; and secondly, since she is so much holier than that angel, and we so much less holy than Daniel, what great reason we have to call her the Virgin Most Admirable, the Wonderful, the [awesome] Virgin, when we think of her ineffable purity!

There are those who are so thoughtless, so blind, so groveling as to think that Mary is not as much shocked at willful sin as her Divine Son is, and that we can make her our friend and advocate, though we go to her without contrition at heart, without even the wish for true repentance and resolution to amend. As if Mary could hate sin less, and love sinners more, than our Lord does! No: she feels a sympathy for those only who wish to *leave* their sins; else, how should she be without sin herself? No: if even to the best of us she is, in the words of Scripture, "fair as the moon, bright as the sun, and *terrible as an army set in array*," what is she to the impenitent sinner? (*Meditations and Devotions*, pp. 11–13.)

House of Gold

WHY IS SHE called *a House?* And why is she called *Golden?*
Gold is the most beautiful, the most valuable, of all metals. Silver, copper, and steel may in their way be made good to the eye, but nothing is so rich, so splendid, as gold. We have few opportunities of seeing it in any quantity; but anyone who has seen a large number of bright gold coins knows how magnificent is the look of gold. Hence it is that in Scripture the Holy City is, by a figure of speech, called golden. "The City," says St. John, "was pure gold, as it were transparent glass." He means of course to give us a notion of the wondrous beautifulness of heaven, by comparing it with what is the most beautiful of all the substances which we see on earth.

Therefore it is that Mary too is called golden; because her graces, her virtues, her innocence, her purity are of that transcendent brilliancy and dazzling perfection, so costly, so exquisite, that the angels cannot, so to say, keep their eyes off her any more than *we* could help gazing upon any great work of gold.

But observe further, she is a golden house, or, I will rather say, a golden palace. Let us imagine we saw a whole palace or large church all made of gold, from the foundations to the roof; such, in regard to the number, the variety, the extent of her spiritual excellencies, is Mary.

But why called a house or palace? And whose palace? She is the house and the palace of the Great King, of God himself. Our Lord, the co-equal Son of God, once dwelt in her. He was her

Guest; nay, more than a guest, for a guest comes into a house as well as leaves it. But our Lord was actually born in this holy house. He took his flesh and his blood from this house, from the flesh, from the veins of Mary. Rightly then was she made to be of pure gold, because she was to give of that gold to form the body of the Son of God. She was golden in her conception, golden in her birth. She went through the fire of her suffering like gold in the furnace, and when she ascended on high, she was, in the words of our hymn,

> Above all the angels in glory untold,
> Standing next to the King in a vesture of gold.

(*Meditations and Devotions,* pp. 14–15.)

Mother Most Amiable

WHY IS SHE "amiable" thus specially? It is because she was without sin. Sin is something odious in its very nature, and grace is something bright, beautiful, attractive.

However, it may be said that sinlessness was not enough to make others love her or to make her dear to others, and that for two reasons: first, because we cannot like anyone that is not like ourselves, and we are sinners; and next, because her being holy would not make her pleasant and winning, because holy persons whom we fall in with, are not always agreeable, and we cannot [always] like them, however we may revere them and look up to them.

Now as to the first of these two questions, we may grant that bad men do not, cannot, like good men; but our Blessed Virgin Mary is called amiable, or lovable, as being such to the children of the Church, not to those outside of it, who know nothing about her. And no child of Holy Church but has some remains of God's grace in his soul which makes him sufficiently like her, however greatly wanting he may be, to allow of his being able to love her. So we may let this question pass.

But as to the second question: How are we sure that our Lady, when she was on earth, attracted people around her and made them love her merely because she was holy?—considering that holy people sometimes have not that gift of drawing others to them.

To explain this point we must recollect that there is a vast difference between the state of a soul such as that of the Blessed Virgin, which has *never* sinned, and a soul, however holy, which has *once* had upon it Adam's sin. For, even after Baptism and Penance, it suffers necessarily from the spiritual wounds which are the consequence of that sin. Holy men, indeed, never commit *mortal* sin,nay, sometimes have never committed even one mortal sin in the whole course of their lives. But Mary's holiness went beyond this. She never committed even a *venial* sin, and this special privilege is not known to belong to anyone but Mary.

Now, whatever want of amiableness, sweetness, attractiveness really exists in holy men arises from the *remains* of sin in them, or again from the want of a holiness powerful enough to overcome the defects of nature, whether of soul or body. But, as to Mary, her holiness was such that if we saw her, and heard her, we should not be able to tell to those who asked us anything about her except simply that she was angelic and heavenly.

Of course her face was most beautiful; but we should not be able to recollect whether it was beautiful or not. We should not recollect any of her features, because it was her beautiful sinless soul, which looked through her eyes, and spoke through her mouth, and was heard in her voice, and compassed her all about. When she was still, or when she walked, whether she smiled or was sad, it was her sinless soul which would draw all those to her who had any grace in them, any remains of grace, any love of holy things. There was a divine music in all she said and did—in her mien, her air, her deportment, that charmed every true heart that came near her. Her innocence, her humility and modesty, her simplicity, sincerity, and truthfulness, her unselfishness, her unaffected interest in everyone who came to her, her purity—it was these qualities which made her so lovable. And were we to see her now, neither our first thought nor our second thought would be what she could do for us with her Son (though she can do so much), but our first thought would be, "Oh, how beautiful!" and our second thought would be, "Oh, what ugly, hateful creatures are we!" (*Meditations and Devotions,* pp. 16–18.)

Mystical Rose

1.

How did Mary become the *Rosa Mystica,* the choice, delicate, perfect flower of God's spiritual creation? It was by being born, nurtured, and sheltered in the mystical garden or Paradise of God. Scripture makes use of the figure of a garden when it would speak of heaven and its blessed inhabitants. A garden is a spot of ground set apart for trees and plants, all good, all various, for things that are sweet to the taste, or fragrant in scent, or beautiful to look upon, or useful for nourishment. Accordingly in its spiritual sense it means the home of blessed spirits and holy souls dwelling there together, souls with both the flowers and the fruits upon them, which by the careful husbandry of God they have come to bear, flowers and fruits of grace, flowers more beautiful and more fragrant than those of any garden, fruits more delicious and exquisite than can be matured by earthly husbandman.

All that God has made speaks of its Maker; the mountains speak of his eternity, the sun of his immensity, and the winds of his almightiness. In like manner flowers and fruits speak of his sanctity, his love, and his providence; and such as are flowers and fruits, such must be the place where they are found. That is to say, since they are found in a garden, therefore a garden has also excellences which speak of God, because it is their home. For instance, it would be out of place if we found beautiful flowers on the mountain crag, or rich fruit in the sandy desert. As then by flowers and fruits are meant, in a mystical sense, the gifts and graces of the

Holy Ghost, so by a garden is meant mystically a place of spiritual repose, stillness, peace, refreshment, and delight.

Our first parents were placed in "a garden of pleasure" shaded by trees, "fair to behold and pleasant to eat of," with the Tree of Life in the midst and a river to water the ground. Thus our Lord, speaking from the cross to the penitent robber, calls the blessed place, the heaven to which he was taking him, "paradise," or a garden of pleasure. Therefore St. John, in the Book of Revelation, speaks of heaven, the palace of God, as a garden or paradise in which was the Tree of Life giving forth its fruits every month.

Such was the garden in which the Mystical Rose, the Immaculate Mary, was sheltered and nursed to be the mother of the All Holy God, from her birth to her espousal to St. Joseph, a term of thirteen years. For three years of it she was in the arms of her holy mother, St. Anne, and then for ten years she lived in the Temple of God. In those blessed gardens, as they may be called, she lived by herself, continually visited by the dew of God's grace, and growing up a more and more heavenly flower, till at the end of that period she was suitable for the inhabitation in her of the Most Holy. This was the outcome of the Immaculate Conception. Excepting her, the fairest rose in the paradise of God has had upon it blight and has had the risk of canker-worm and locust. All but Mary; she from the first was perfect in her sweetness and her beautifulness, and at length when the angel Gabriel came to her he found her "full of grace," which had, from her good use of it, accumulated in her from the first moment of her being. (*Meditations and Devotions*, pp. 19–21.)

2.

MARY IS THE most beautiful flower that ever was seen in the spiritual world. It is by the power of God's grace that from this barren and desolate earth there have ever sprung up at all flowers of holiness and glory. And Mary is the queen of them. She is the queen of spiritual flowers; and therefore she is called the *rose,* for the rose is fitly called of all flowers the most beautiful.

But moreover, she is the *mystical,* or *hidden* rose; for mystical means hidden. How is she now "hidden" from us more than are other saints? What means this singular appellation, which we apply to her specially? The answer to this question introduces us to a third reason for believing in the reunion of her sacred body to her soul, and its assumption into heaven soon after her death, instead of its lingering in the grave until the general resurrection at the last day.

It is this: if her body was not taken into heaven, where is it? How comes it that it is hidden from us? Why do we not hear of her tomb as being here or there? Why are not pilgrimages made to it? Why are not relics producible of her, as of the saints in general? Is it not even a natural instinct which makes us reverent towards the places where our dead are buried? We bury our great men honorably. St. Peter speaks of the sepulcher of David as known in his day, though he had died many hundred years before. When our Lord's body was taken down from the cross, he was placed in an honorable tomb. Such too had been the honor already paid to St. John the Baptist, his tomb being spoken of by St. Mark as generally known. Christians from the earliest times went from other countries to Jerusalem to see the holy places. And, when the time of persecution was over, they paid still more attention to the bodies of the saints, as of St. Stephen, St. Mark, St. Barnabas, St. Peter, St. Paul, and other apostles and martyrs. These were transported to great cities, and portions of them sent to this place or that. Thus, from the first to this day it has been a great feature and characteristic of the Church to be most tender and reverent towards the bodies of the saints.

Now, if there was anyone who more than all would be preciously taken care of, it would be our Lady. Why then do we hear nothing of the Blessed Virgin's body and its separate relics? Why is she thus the *hidden* rose? Is it conceivable that they who had been so reverent and careful of the bodies of the saints and martyrs should neglect her—her who was the Queen of Martyrs and the Queen of Saints, who was the very Mother of our Lord? It is impossible. Why then is she thus the *hidden* rose? Plainly because that sacred body is in heaven, not on earth. (*Meditations and Devotions*, pp. 65–67.)

Virgin Most Venerable

WE USE the word "venerable" generally for what is *old*. That is because only what is old has commonly those qualities which excite reverence or veneration.

It is a great history, a great character, a maturity of virtue, goodness, experience, that excite our reverence, and these commonly cannot belong to the young.

But this is not true when we are considering saints. A short life with them is a long one. Thus Holy Scripture says, "Venerable age is not that of long time, nor counted by the number of years, but it is the *understanding* of a man that is grey hairs, and a spotless life is old age. The just man, if he be cut short by death, shall be at rest; being made perfect in a short time, he fulfilled a long time."

Nay, there is a heathen writer, who knew nothing of saints, who lays it down that even to children, to all children, a great reverence should be paid, and that on the ground of their being as yet innocent. And this is a feeling very widely felt and expressed in all countries; so much so that the sight of those who have not sinned (that is, who are not yet old enough to have fallen into mortal sin) has, on the very score of that innocent, smiling youthfulness, often disturbed and turned aside the plunderer or the assassin in the midst of his guilty doings—filled him with a sudden fear and brought him, if not to repentance, at least to change of purpose.

And, to pass from the thought of the lowest to the highest, what shall we say of the Eternal God (if we may safely speak of him at all) but that he, *because* he is eternal, is ever *young*, without a beginning, and therefore without change, and, in the fullness and perfection of his incomprehensible attributes, now just what he was a million years ago? He is truly called in Scripture the "Ancient of Days," and is therefore infinitely venerable. Yet he needs not old age to make him venerable. He has really nothing of those human attendants on venerableness which the sacred writers are obliged figuratively to ascribe to him, in order to make us feel that profound abasement and that reverential awe which we ought to entertain at the thought of him.

And so of the great Mother of God, as far as a creature can be like the Creator, her ineffable purity and utter freedom from any shadow of sin, her Immaculate Conception, her ever-virginity— these her prerogatives (in spite of her extreme youth at the time when Gabriel came to her) are such as to lead us to exclaim in the prophetic words of Scripture, both with awe and with exaltation: "Thou art the glory of Jerusalem and the joy of Israel; thou art the honor of our people; therefore hath the hand of the Lord strengthened thee, and therefore art thou blessed forever." (*Meditations and Devotions*, pp. 22–24.)

Holy Mary

G OD ALONE can claim the attribute of holiness. Hence we say in the hymn: *"Tu solus sanctus"* (Thou only art holy). By holiness we mean the absence of whatever sullies, dims, and degrades a rational nature, all that is most opposite and contrary to sin and guilt.

We say that God alone is holy, though in truth all his high attributes are possessed by him in that fullness, that it may be truly said that he alone has them. Thus, as to goodness, our Lord said to the young man, "None is good but God alone." He too alone is power, he alone is wisdom, he alone is providence, love, mercy, justice, truth. This is true; but holiness is singled out as his special prerogative because it marks more than his other attributes, not only his superiority over all his creatures, but emphatically his separation from them. Hence we read in the Book of Job, "Can man be justified compared with God, or he that is born of a woman appear clean? Behold, even the moon doth not shine, and the stars are not pure, in his sight." "Behold, among his saints none is unchangeable, and the heavens are not pure in his sight."

This we must receive and understand in the first place; but secondly we know too, that, in his mercy, he has communicated in various measures his great attributes to his rational creatures, and, first of all, as being most necessary, holiness. Thus Adam, from the time of his creation, was gifted, over and above his nature as man, with the grace of God, to unite him to God and to make him holy. Grace is therefore called holy grace; and, as being holy, it is the connecting principle between God and man. Adam in Paradise might have had knowledge, and skill, and many virtues; but these gifts did not unite him to his Creator. It was holiness that united him, for it is said by St. Paul, "Without holiness no man shall see God."

And so again, when man fell and lost this holy grace, he had various gifts still adhering to him. He might be, in a certain measure, true, merciful, loving, and just; but these virtues did not unite him to God. What he needed was holiness. And therefore the first act of God's goodness to us in the Gospel is to take us out of our unholy state by means of the Sacrament of Baptism, and by the grace then given us to reopen the communications, so long closed, between the soul and heaven.

We see then the force of our Lady's title, when we call her "Holy Mary." When God wanted to prepare a human mother for his Son, he began by giving her an immaculate conception. He began, not by giving her the gift of love, or truthfulness, or gentleness, or devotion, though according to the occasion she had them all, but he began his great work before she was born, before she could think, speak, or act, by making her holy, and thereby, while on earth, a citizen of heaven. *"Tota pulchra es, Maria!"* Nothing of the deformity of sin was ever hers. Thus she differs from all saints. There have been great missionaries, confessors, bishops, doctors, pastors. They have done great works and have taken with them numberless converts or penitents to heaven. They have suffered much and have a superabundance of merits to show. But Mary in this way resembles her Divine Son: as he, being God, is separate by holiness from all creatures, so she is separate from all saints and angels, as being "full of grace." (*Meditations and Devotions,* pp. 25–27.

Queen of Angels

THIS GREAT TITLE may be fitly connected with the maternity of Mary, that is, with the coming upon her of the Holy Ghost at Nazareth after the angel Gabriel's annunciation to her, and with the consequent birth of our Lord at Bethlehem. She, as the Mother of our Lord, comes nearer to him than any angel; nearer even than the Seraphim who surround him and cry continually, "Holy, Holy, Holy."

The two archangels who have a special office in the Gospel are St. Gabriel and St. Michael—and both of them are associated in the history of the Incarnation with Mary: St. Gabriel, when the Holy Ghost came down upon her; and St. Michael, when the Divine Child was born.

St. Gabriel hailed her as "full of grace," and as "blessed among women," and announced to her that the Holy Ghost would come down upon her, and that she would bear a Son who would be the Son of the Highest.

Of St. Michael's ministry to her, on the birth of that Divine Son, we learn in the Book of Revelation, written by the apostle St. John. We know our Lord came to set up the Kingdom of Heaven among men, and hardly was he born when he was assaulted by the powers of the world who wished to destroy him. Herod sought to take his life, but he was defeated by St. Joseph's carrying his Mother and him off into Egypt. But St. John in the Book of Revelation tells us that Michael and his angels were the real guardians of Mother and Child, then and on other occasions. First,

St. John saw in vision "a great sign in heaven" (meaning by "heaven," the Church, or Kingdom of God), "a woman clothed with the sun, and with the moon under her feet, and on her head a crown of twelve stars"; and when she was about to be delivered of her Child there appeared "a great red dragon," that is, the evil spirit, ready "to devour her Son" when he should be born. The Son was preserved by his own divine power, but next the evil spirit persecuted her. St. Michael, however, and his angels came to the rescue and prevailed against him. "There was a great battle," says the sacred writer: "Michael and his angels fought with the dragon, and the dragon fought and his angels; and that great dragon was cast out, the old serpent, who is called the devil." Now, as then, the Blessed Mother of God has hosts of angels who do her service, and she is their queen. (*Meditations and Devotions,* pp. 28–29.)

Mirror of Justice

HERE FIRST we must consider what is meant by justice, for the word as used by the Church has not that sense which it bears in ordinary English. By "justice" is not meant the virtue of fairness, equity, uprightness in our dealings. It is a word denoting all virtues at once, a perfect, virtuous state of soul—righteousness, or moral perfection; so that it answers very nearly to what is meant by sanctity. Therefore when our Lady is called the "Mirror of Justice," it is meant to say that she is the mirror of sanctity, holiness, supernatural goodness.

Next, what is meant by calling her a mirror? A mirror is a surface which reflects, as still water, polished steel, or a looking-glass. What did Mary reflect? She reflected our Lord—but he is infinite sanctity. She then, as far as a creature could, reflected his divine sanctity, and therefore she is the mirror of sanctity or, as the Litany says, of justice.

Do we ask how she came to reflect his sanctity?—it was by living with him. We see every day how like people get to each other who live with those they love. When they live with those whom they don't love, as, for instance, the members of a family who quarrel with each other, then the longer they live together the more unlike each other they become. But when they love each other, as husband and wife, parents and children, brothers with brothers or sisters, friends with friends, then in course of time they get surprisingly like each other. All of us perceive this. We are witnesses to it with our own eyes and ears. In the expression of their features, in their voice, in their walk, in their language, even in their handwriting, they become like each other—and so with regard to their minds, as in their opinions, their tastes, their pursuits. And again doubtless in the state of their souls, which we do not see, whether for good or for bad.

Now, consider that Mary loved her Divine Son with an unutterable love; and consider too she had him all to herself for thirty years. Do we not see that, as she was full of grace before she conceived him in her womb, she must have had a vast incomprehensible sanctity when she had lived close to God for thirty years?— a sanctity of an angelical order, reflecting back the attributes of God with a fullness and exactness of which no saint upon earth, or hermit, or holy virgin, can even remind us. Truly then she is the Mirror of Justice, the Mirror of Divine Perfection. (*Meditations and Devotions,* pp. 30–31.)

Seat of Wisdom

M ARY HAS this title in her Litany because the Son of God, who is also called in Scripture the Word and Wisdom of God, once dwelt in her, and then, after his birth of her, was carried in her arms and seated in her lap in his first years. Thus, being as it were, the human throne of him who reigns in heaven, she is called the Seat of Wisdom. In the poet's words:

> His throne, thy bosom blest,
>   O Mother undefiled,
> That throne, if aught beneath the skies,
>   Beseems the sinless Child.

But the possession of her Son lasted beyond his infancy—he was under her rule, as St. Luke tells us, and lived with her in her house, till he went forth to preach—that is, for at least a whole thirty years. And this brings us to a reflection about her, cognate to that which was suggested to us yesterday by the title of "Mirror of Justice." For if such close and continued intimacy with her Son created in her a sanctity inconceivably great, must not also the knowledge which she gained during those many years from his conversation of present, past, and future have been so large, and so profound, and so diversified, and so thorough, that, though she was a poor woman without human advantages, she must in her knowledge of creation, of the universe, and of history have excelled the greatest of philosophers, and in her theological knowledge the greatest of theologians, and in her prophetic discernment the most favored of prophets?

What was the grand theme of conversation between her and her Son but the nature, the attributes, the providence, and the works of Almighty God? Would not our Lord be ever glorifying the Father who sent him? Would he not unfold to her the solemn eternal decrees, and the purposes, and will of God? Would he not from time to time enlighten her in all those points of doctrine which have been first discussed and then settled in the Church from the time of the apostles till now, and all that shall be till the end—nay, these, and far more than these? All that is obscure, all that is fragmentary in revelation, would, so far as the knowledge is possible to man, be brought out to her in clearness and simplicity by him who is the Light of the World.

And so of the events which are to come. God spoke to the prophets; we have his communications to them in Scripture. But he spoke to them in figure and parable. There was one, Moses, to whom he vouchsafed to speak face to face. "If there be among you a prophet of the Lord," God says, "I will appear to him in a vision, and I will speak to him in a dream. But it is not so with my servant Moses . . . For I will speak to him mouth to mouth and plainly, and not by riddles and figures doth he see the Lord." This was the great privilege of the inspired lawgiver of the Jews; but how much was it below that of Mary! Moses had the privilege only now and then, from time to time. But Mary for thirty continuous years saw and heard him, being all through that time face to face with him, and being able to ask him any question which she wished explained, and knowing that the answers she received were from the Eternal God, who neither deceives nor can be deceived. (*Meditations and Devotions*, pp. 32–34.)

Gate of Heaven

M ARY IS CALLED the Gate of Heaven because it was through her that our Lord passed from heaven to earth. The prophet Ezekiel, prophesying of Mary, says, "The gate shall be closed, it shall not be opened, and no man shall pass through it, since the Lord God of Israel has entered through it—and it shall be closed for the Prince, the Prince himself shall sit in it."

Now this is fulfilled, not only in our Lord having taken flesh from her, and being her Son, but moreover, in that she had a place in the economy of redemption. It is fulfilled in her spirit and will, as well as in her body. Eve had a part in the fall of man, though it was Adam who was our representative, and whose sin made us sinners. It was Eve who began, and who tempted Adam. Scripture says: "The woman saw that the tree was good to eat, and fair to the eyes, and delightful to behold; and she took of the fruit thereof, and did eat, and gave to her husband, and he did eat." It was fitting then in God's mercy that, as the woman began the destruction of the world, so woman should also begin its recovery. And as Eve opened the way for the fatal deed of the first Adam, so Mary should open the way for the great achievement of the second Adam, our Lord Jesus Christ himself, who came to save the world by dying on the cross for it. Hence Mary is called by the holy Fathers a second and a better Eve, as having taken that first step in the salvation of mankind which Eve took in its ruin.

How, and when, did Mary take part, and the initial part, in the world's restoration? It was when the angel Gabriel came to her to announce to her the great dignity which was to be her portion. St. Paul bids us "present our bodies to God as a reasonable service." We must not only pray with our lips, and fast, and do outward penance, and be chaste in our bodies; but we must be obedient, and pure in our minds. And so, as regards the Blessed Virgin, it was God's will that she should undertake willingly and with full understanding to be the Mother of our Lord, and not to be a mere passive instrument whose maternity would have no merit and no reward. The higher our gifts, the heavier our duties. It was no light lot to be so intimately near to the Redeemer of men, as she experienced afterwards when she suffered with him. Therefore, weighing well the angel's words before giving her answer to them—first she asked whether so great an office would be a forfeiture of that virginity which she had vowed. When the angel told her no, then, with the full consent of a full heart, full of God's love to her and her own lowliness, she said, "Behold the handmaid of the Lord, be it done unto me according to thy word." It was by this consent that she became the *Gate of Heaven*. (*Meditations and Devotions*, pp. 35–37.)

Mother of the Creator

THIS IS a title which, of all others, we should have thought it impossible for any creature to possess. At first sight we might be tempted to say that it throws into confusion our primary ideas of the Creator and the creature, the Eternal and the temporal, the Self-subsisting and the dependent. Yet on further consideration we shall see that we cannot refuse the title to Mary without denying the divine Incarnation—that is, the great and fundamental truth of revelation, that God became man.

And this was seen from the first age of the Church. Christians were accustomed from the first to call the Blessed Virgin the "Mother of God," because they saw that it was impossible to deny her that title without denying St. John's words, "The Word" (that is, God the Son) "was made flesh."

And before long it was found necessary to proclaim this truth by the voice of an Ecumenical Council of the Church. For, in consequence of the dislike which men have of a mystery, the error sprang up that our Lord was not really God, but a man, differing from us in this merely—that God dwelt in him, as God dwells in all good men, only in a higher measure. That God dwelt in him as the Holy Spirit dwelt in angels and prophets, as in a sort of temple; or again, as our Lord now dwells in the tabernacle in church. And then the bishops and faithful people found there was no other way of hindering this false, bad view being taught, but by declaring distinctly, and making it a point of faith, that Mary was the mother, not of man only, but of God. And since that time the title of Mary, as Mother of God, has become what is called a dogma, or article of faith, in the Church.

But this leads us to a larger view of the subject. Is this title as given to Mary more wonderful than the doctrine that God, without ceasing to be God, should become man? Is it more mysterious that Mary should be Mother of God, than that God should be man? Yet the latter, as I have said, is the elementary truth of revelation, witnessed by prophets, evangelists, and apostles all through Scripture.

And what can be more consoling and joyful than the wonderful promises which follow from this truth, that Mary is the Mother of God?—the great wonder, namely, that we become the brethren of our God; that, if we live well, and die in the grace of God, we shall all of us hereafter be taken up by our Incarnate God to that place where angels dwell; that our bodies shall be raised from the dust and be taken to heaven; that we shall be really united to God; that we shall be partakers of the divine nature; that each of us, soul and body, shall be plunged into the abyss of glory which surrounds the Almighty; that we shall see him and share his blessedness, according to the text, "Whosoever shall do the will of my Father that is in heaven, the same is my brother, and sister, and mother." (*Meditations and Devotions,* pp. 38–40.)

Mother of Christ

E ACH OF the titles of Mary has its own special meaning and
drift, and may be made the subject of a distinct meditation.
She is invoked by us as the Mother of Christ. What is the force of
thus addressing her? It is to bring before us that she it is who from
the first was prophesied of and associated with the hopes and
prayers of all holy men, of all true worshippers of God, of all who
"looked for the redemption of Israel" in every age before that redemption came.

Our Lord was called the Christ, or the Messiah, by the Jewish prophets and the Jewish people. The two words "Christ" and
"Messiah" mean the same. They mean in English the "Anointed."
In the old time there were three great ministries or offices by
means of which God spoke to his chosen people, the Israelites, or,
as they were afterwards called, the Jews—that of priest, that of
king, and that of prophet. Those who were chosen by God for
one or other of these offices were solemnly anointed with oil—
oil signifying the grace of God, which was given to them for the
due performance of their high duties. But our Lord was all three,
a priest, a prophet, and a king—a priest, because he offered himself as a sacrifice for our sins; a prophet, because he revealed to us
the Holy Law of God; and a king, because he rules over us. Thus
he is the one true Christ.

It was in expectation of this great Messiah that the chosen
people, the Jews, or Israelites, or Hebrews (for these are different
names for the same people), looked out from age to age. He was

to come to set all things right. And next to this great question
which occupied their minds, namely, when was he to come, was
the question, who was to be his Mother? It had been told them
from the first, not that he should come from heaven, but that he
should be born of a woman. At the time of the fall of Adam, God
had said that the seed of the Woman should bruise the Serpent's
head.

Who, then, was to be that Woman thus significantly pointed
out to the fallen race of Adam? At the end of many centuries it
was further revealed to the Jews that the great Messiah or Christ,
the seed of the Woman, should be born of their race, and of one
particular tribe of the twelve tribes into which that race was divided. From that time every woman of that tribe hoped to have
the great privilege of herself being the mother of the Messiah, or
Christ; for it stood to reason, since he was so great, the mother
must be great, and good, and blessed too. Hence it was, among
other reasons, that they thought so highly of the marriage state,
because, not knowing the mystery of the miraculous conception
of the Christ when he was actually to come, they thought that the
marriage rite was the ordinance necessary for his coming.

Hence it was, if Mary had been as other women, she would
have longed for marriage as opening on her the prospect of bear-
ing the great King. But she was too humble and too pure for such
thoughts. She had been inspired to choose that better way of serving God which had not been made known to the Jews—the state
of virginity. She preferred to be his spouse to being his mother.
Accordingly, when the angel Gabriel announced to her her high
destiny, she shrank from it till she was assured that it would not
oblige her to revoke her purpose of a virgin life devoted to her
God.

Thus was it that she became the mother of the Christ, not in
that way which pious women for so many ages had expected him,

but, declining the grace of such maternity, she gained it by means of a higher grace. And this is the full meaning of St. Elizabeth's words, when the Blessed Virgin came to visit her, which we use in the Hail Mary: "Blessed art thou among women, and blessed is the fruit of thy womb." And therefore it is that in the devotion called the "Crown of Twelve Stars" we give praise to God the Holy Ghost, through whom she was both Virgin and Mother. (*Meditations and Devotions*, pp. 41–43.)

Mother of the Savior

HERE AGAIN, as in our reflections of yesterday, we must understand what is meant by calling our Lord a Savior, in order to understand why it is used to form one of the titles given to Mary in her Litany.

The special name by which our Lord was known before his coming was, as we found yesterday, that of Messiah, or Christ. Thus he was known to the Jews. But when he actually showed himself on earth, he was known by three new titles, the Son of God, the Son of Man, and the Savior. The first was expressive of his divine nature, the second of his human, the third of his personal office. Thus the angel who appeared to Mary called him the Son of God; the angel who appeared to Joseph called him Jesus, which means in English *Savior;* and so the angels, too, called him a Savior when they appeared to the shepherds. But he himself specially calls himself the Son of Man.

Not angels only called him Savior, but those two greatest of the apostles, St. Peter and St. Paul, in their first preachings. St. Peter says he is "a Prince and a Savior," and St. Paul says, "a Savior, Jesus." And both angels and apostles tell us why he is so called—because he has rescued us from the power of the evil spirit, and from the guilt and misery of our sins. Thus the angel says to Joseph, "Thou shalt call his name Jesus, for he shall save his people from their sins"; and St. Peter, "God has exalted him to be Prince and Savior, to give repentance to Israel, and remission of sins." And Jesus says himself, "The Son of Man is come to seek and to save that which is lost."

Now let us consider how this affects our thoughts of Mary. To rescue slaves from the power of the enemy implies a conflict. Our Lord, because he was a Savior, was a warrior. He could not deliver the captives without a fight, nor without personal suffering. Now, who are they who especially hate wars? A heathen poet answers: "Wars," he says, "are hated by mothers." Mothers are precisely those who especially suffer in a war. They may glory in the honor gained by their children, but still such glorying does not wipe out one particle of the long pain, the anxiety, the suspense, the desolation, and the anguish which the mother of a soldier feels.

So it was with Mary. For thirty years she was blessed with the continual presence of her Son—nay, she had him in subjection. But the time came when that war called for him for which he had come upon earth. Certainly he came, not simply to be the Son of Mary, but to be the Savior of Man, and therefore at length he parted from her. She knew then what it was to be the mother of a soldier. He left her side; she saw him no longer; she tried in vain to get near him. He had for years lived in her embrace, and after that, at least in her dwelling—but now, in his own words, "The Son of Man had nowhere to lay his head." And then, when years had run out, she heard of his arrest, his mock trial, and his Passion.

At last she got near him—when and where?—on the way to Calvary, and when he had been lifted upon the cross. And at length she held him again in her arms; yes—when he was dead. True, he rose from the dead, but still she did not thereby gain him, for he ascended on high, and she did not at once follow him. No, she remained on earth many years—in the care, indeed, of his dearest apostle, St. John. But what was even the holiest of men compared with her own son, and him the Son of God? O Holy Mary, Mother of our Savior, in this meditation we have now suddenly passed from the Joyful Mysteries to the Sorrowful, from Gabriel's Annunciation to thee, to the Seven Dolors. That, then, will be the next series of meditations which we make about thee. (*Meditations and Devotions,* pp. 44–46.)

Queen of Martyrs

WHY IS SHE SO called?—she who never had any blow, or wound, or other injury to her consecrated person. How can she be exalted over those whose bodies suffered the most ruthless violence and the keenest torments for our Lord's sake? She is, indeed, Queen of all Saints, of those who "walk with Christ in white, for they are worthy"; but how [is she queen] of those "who were slain for the Word of God, and for the testimony which they held"?

To answer this question, it must be recollected that the pains of the soul may be as fierce as those of the body. Bad men who are now in hell, and the elect of God who are in purgatory, are suffering only in their souls, for their bodies are still in the dust; yet how severe is that suffering! And perhaps most people who have lived long can bear witness in their own persons to a sharpness of distress which was like a sword cutting them, to a weight and force of sorrow which seemed to throw them down, though bodily pain there was none.

What an overwhelming horror it must have been for the Blessed Mary to witness the Passion and the Crucifixion of her Son! Her anguish was, as holy Simeon had announced to her, at the time of her Son's presentation in the Temple, a sword piercing her soul. If our Lord himself could not bear the prospect of what was before him, and was covered at the thought of it with a bloody sweat, his soul thus acting upon his body, does not this show how great mental pain can be? And would it have been a thing to wonder at if Mary's head and heart had given way as she stood under his cross?

Thus is she most truly the Queen of *Martyrs*. (*Meditations and Devotions*, pp. 47–48.)

Singular Vessel of Devotion

To be devout is to be devoted. We know what is meant by a devoted wife or daughter. It is one whose thoughts center in the person so deeply loved, so tenderly cherished. She follows him about with her eyes; she is ever seeking some means of serving him. And, if her services are very small in their character, that only shows how intimate they are, and how incessant. And especially if the object of her love be weak, or in pain, or near to die, still more intensely does she live in his life and know nothing but him.

This intense devotion towards our Lord, forgetting self in love for him, is instanced in St. Paul, who says, "I know nothing but Jesus Christ and him crucified." And again, "I live, [yet] now not I, but Christ liveth in me; and [the life] that I now live in the flesh, I live in the faith of the Son of God, who loved me, and delivered himself for me."

But great as was St. Paul's devotion to our Lord, much greater was that of the Blessed Virgin; because she was his Mother, and because she had him and all his sufferings actually before her eyes, and because she had the long intimacy of thirty years with him, and because she was from her special sanctity so ineffably near to him in spirit. When, then, he was mocked, bruised, scourged, and nailed to the cross, she felt as keenly as if every indignity and torture inflicted on him was struck at herself. She could have cried out in agony at every pang of his.

This is called her *compassion*, or her suffering with her Son, and it arose from this that she was the "Singular Vessel of Devotion." (*Meditations and Devotions*, pp. 49–50.)

Vessel of Honor

S T. PAUL CALLS elect souls vessels of honor: of honor, because they are elect or chosen; and vessels, because, through the love of God, they are filled with God's heavenly and holy grace. How much more then is Mary a vessel of honor by reason of her having within her, not only the grace of God, but the very Son of God, formed as regards his flesh and blood out of her!

But this title "of honor," as applied to Mary, admits of a further and special meaning. She was a martyr without the rude dishonor which accompanied the sufferings of the martyrs. The martyrs were seized, haled about, thrust into prison with the vilest criminals, and assailed with the most blasphemous words and foulest speeches which Satan could inspire. Nay, such was the unutterable trial also of the holy women, young ladies, the spouses of Christ, whom the heathen seized, tortured, and put to death. Above all, our Lord himself, whose sanctity was greater than any created excellence or vessel of grace—even he, as we know well, was buffeted, stripped, scourged, mocked, dragged about, and then stretched, nailed, lifted up on a high cross, to the gaze of a brutal multitude.

But he, who bore the sinner's shame for sinners, spared his Mother, who was sinless, this supreme indignity. Not in the body, but in the soul, she suffered. True, in his agony she was agonized; in his Passion she suffered a fellow-passion; she was crucified with him; the spear that pierced his breast pierced through her spirit. Yet there were no visible signs of this intimate martyrdom. She stood up, still, collected, motionless, solitary, under the cross of her Son, surrounded by angels, and shrouded in her virginal sanctity from the notice of all who were taking part in his Crucifixion. (*Meditations and Devotions*, pp. 51–52.)

Spiritual Vessel

To be spiritual is to live in the world of spirits. As St. Paul says, "Our conversation is in heaven." To be spiritually minded is to see by faith all those good and holy beings who actually surround us, though we see them not with our bodily eyes; to see them by faith as vividly as we see the things of earth—the green country, the blue sky, and the brilliant sunshine. Hence it is that, when saintly souls are favored with heavenly visions, these visions are but the extraordinary continuations and the crown, by a divine intuition, of objects which, by the ordinary operation of grace, are ever before their minds. These visions consoled and strengthened the Blessed Virgin in all her sorrows. The angels who were around her understood her, and she understood them, with a directness which is not to be expected in their intercourse with us who have inherited from Adam the taint of sin. Doubtless; but still let us never forget that as she in her sorrows was comforted by angels, so it is our privilege in the many trials of life to be comforted, in our degree, by the same heavenly messengers of the Most High; nay, by Almighty God himself, the third Person of the Holy Trinity, who has taken on himself the office of being our Paraclete, or Present Help.

Let all those who are in trouble take this comfort to themselves, if they are trying to lead a spiritual life. If they call on God, he will answer them. Though they have no earthly friend, they have him, who, as he felt for his Mother when he was on the cross, now that he is in his glory feels for the lowest and feeblest of his people. (*Meditations and Devotions*, pp. 53–54.)

Comforter of the Afflicted

S T. PAUL SAYS that his Lord comforted him in all his tribulation, that he also might be able to comfort them who are in distress, by the encouragement which he received from God. This is the secret of true consolation: those are able to comfort others who in their own case have been much tried, and have felt the need of consolation, and have received it. So of our Lord himself it is said: "In that he himself hath suffered and been tempted, he is able to succor those also that are tempted."

And this too is why the Blessed Virgin is the comforter of the afflicted. We all know how special a mother's consolation is, and we are allowed to call Mary our mother from the time that our Lord from the cross established the relation of mother and son between her and St. John. And she especially can console us because she suffered more than mothers in general.

Women, at least delicate women, are commonly shielded from rude experience of the highways of the world; but she, after our Lord's Ascension, was sent out into foreign lands almost as the apostles were, a sheep among wolves. In spite of all St. John's care of her, which was as great as was St. Joseph's in her younger days, she, more than all the saints of God, was a stranger and a pilgrim upon earth, in proportion to her greater love of him who had been on earth and had gone away. As, when our Lord was an infant she had to flee across the desert to heathen Egypt, so when he had ascended on high, she had to go on shipboard to the heathen city of Ephesus, where she lived and died. O ye who are in the midst of rude neighbors, or scoffing companions, or of wicked acquaintance, or of spiteful enemies, and are helpless, invoke the aid of Mary by the memory of her own sufferings among the heathen Greek and the heathen Egyptians. (*Meditations and Devotions,* pp. 55–56.)

Virgin Most Prudent

IT MAY NOT appear at first sight how the virtue of prudence is connected with the trials and sorrows of our Lady's life; yet there is a point of view from which we are reminded of her prudence by those trials. It must be recollected that she is not only the great instance of the contemplative life, but also of the practical; and the practical life is at once a life of penance and of prudence, if it is to be well discharged.

Now Mary was as full of external work and hard service as any Sister of Charity of this day. Of course her duties varied according to the seasons of her life, as a young maiden, as a wife, as a mother, and as a widow; but still her life was full of duties day by day and hour by hour. As a stranger in Egypt, she had duties towards the poor heathen among whom she was thrown. As a dweller in Nazareth, she had her duties towards her kinsfolk and neighbors. She had her duties, though unrecorded, during those years in which our Lord was preaching and proclaiming his Kingdom. After he had left this earth, she had her duties towards the apostles, and especially towards the evangelists. She had duties towards the martyrs, and to the confessors in prison; to the sick, to the ignorant, and to the poor. Afterwards, she had to seek with St. John another and a heathen country, where her happy death took place.

But before that death how much must she have suffered in her life amid an idolatrous population! Doubtless the angels screened her eyes from the worst crimes there committed. Still, she was full of duties there—and in consequence she was full of merit. All her acts were perfect, all were the best that could be done. Now, always to be awake, guarded, fervent, so as to be able to act not only without sin, but in the best possible way, in the varying circumstances of each day, denotes a life of untiring mindfulness. But of such a life, prudence is the presiding virtue. It is, then, through the pains and sorrows of her earthly pilgrimage that we are able to invoke her as the *Virgo prudentissima* [Virgin Most Prudent]. (*Meditations and Devotions*, pp. 57–58.)

Tower of Ivory

A TOWER IS a structure which rises higher and is more conspicuous than other objects in its neighborhood. Thus, when we say a man "towers" over his fellows, we mean to signify that they look small in comparison with him.

This quality of greatness is to be found in the Blessed Virgin. Though she suffered more keen and intimate anguish at our Lord's Passion and Crucifixion than any of the apostles by reason of her being his mother, yet consider how much more noble she was amid her deep distress than they were. When our Lord underwent his agony, they slept for sorrow. They could not wrestle with their deep disappointment and despondency; they could not master it; it confused, numbed, and overcame their senses. And soon after, when St. Peter was asked by bystanders whether he was not one of our Lord's disciples, he denied it.

Nor was he alone in this cowardice. The apostles, one and all, forsook our Lord and fled, though St. John returned. Nay, still further, they even lost faith in him and thought all the great expectations which he had raised in them had ended in failure. How different was this even from the brave conduct of St. Mary Magdalen! and still more from that of the Virgin Mother! It is expressly noted of her that she stood by the cross. She did not grovel in the dust, but stood upright to receive the blows, the stabs, which the long Passion of her Son inflicted upon her every moment.

In this magnanimity and generosity in suffering she is as compared with the apostles, fitly imaged as a tower. But towers, it may be said, are huge, rough, heavy, obtrusive, graceless structures, for the purposes of war, not of peace; with nothing of the beautifulness, refinement, and finish which are conspicuous in Mary. It is true: therefore she is called the Tower of Ivory, to suggest to us, by the brightness, purity, and exquisiteness of that material, how transcendent is the loveliness and the gentleness of the Mother of God. (*Meditations and Devotions,* pp. 59–60.)

Holy Mother of God

As SOON AS we apprehend by faith the great fundamental truth that Mary is the Mother of God, other wonderful truths follow in its train. One of these is that she was exempt from the ordinary lot of mortals; which is not only to die, but to become earth to earth, ashes to ashes, dust to dust. Die she must, and die she did, as her Divine Son died, for he was man. But various reasons have approved themselves to holy writers why, although her body was for a while separated from her soul, and consigned to the tomb, yet it did not remain there, but was speedily united to her soul again, and raised by our Lord to a new and eternal life of heavenly glory.

And the most obvious reason for so concluding is this—that other servants of God have been raised from the grave by the power of God, and is it to be supposed that our Lord would have granted any such privilege to anyone else without also granting it to his own Mother?

We are told by St. Matthew that after our Lord's death upon the cross "the graves were opened, and many bodies of the saints that had slept"—that is, slept the sleep of death—"arose, and coming out of the tombs after his Resurrection, came into the Holy City, and appeared to many." St. Matthew says, "*many* bodies of the saints"—that is, the holy prophets, priests, and kings of former times—rose again in anticipation of the last day.

Can we suppose that Abraham, or David, or Isaiah, or Ezekiel should have been thus favored, and not God's own Mother? Had she not a claim on the love of her Son to have what any others had? Was she not nearer to him than the greatest of the saints before her? And is it conceivable that the law of the grave should admit of relaxation in their case, and not in hers? Therefore we confidently say that our Lord, having preserved her from sin and the consequences of sin by his Passion, lost no time in pouring out the full merits of that Passion upon her body as well as her soul. (*Meditations and Devotions,* pp. 61–62.)

Mother Undefiled

A NOTHER CONSIDERATION which has led devout minds to believe in the Assumption of our Lady into heaven after her death, without waiting for the general resurrection at the last day, is furnished by the doctrine of her Immaculate Conception.

By her Immaculate Conception is meant, that not only did she never commit any sin whatever, even venial, in thoughts, word, or deed, but further than this, that the guilt of Adam, or what is called original sin, never was her guilt, as it is the guilt attaching to all other descendants of Adam.

By her Assumption is meant that not only her soul, but her body also, was taken up to heaven upon her death, so that there was no long period of her sleeping in the grave, as is the case with others, even great saints, who wait for the last day for the resurrection of their bodies.

One reason for believing in our Lady's Assumption is that her Divine Son loved her too much to let her body remain in the grave. A second reason—that now is before us—is this, that she was not only dear to our Lord as a mother is dear to a son, but also that she was so transcendently holy, so full, so overflowing with grace. Adam and Eve were created upright and sinless, and had a large measure of God's grace bestowed upon them, and in consequence, their bodies would never have crumbled into dust had they not sinned; upon which it was said to them, "Dust thou art, and unto dust thou shalt return."

If Eve, the beautiful daughter of God, never would have become dust and ashes unless she had sinned, shall we not say that

121

Mary, having never sinned, retained the gift which Eve by sinning lost? What had Mary done to forfeit the privilege given to our first parents in the beginning? Was her comeliness to be turned into corruption, and her fine gold to become dim, without reason assigned? Impossible. Therefore we believe that, though she died for a short hour, as did our Lord himself, yet, like him, and by his almighty power, she was raised again from the grave. (*Meditations and Devotions*, pp. 63–64.)

Tower of David

A TOWER in its simplest idea is a fabric for defense against enemies. David, King of Israel, built for this purpose a notable tower; and as he is a figure or type of our Lord, so is his tower a figure denoting our Lord's Virgin Mother.

She is called the Tower of David because she had so signally fulfilled the office of defending her Divine Son from the assaults of his foes. It is customary with those who are not Catholics to fancy that the honors we pay to her interfere with the supreme worship which we pay to him; that in Catholic teaching she eclipses him. But this is the very reverse of the truth.

For if Mary's glory is so very great, how cannot his be greater still who is the Lord and God of Mary? He is infinitely above his Mother; and all that grace which filled her is but the overflowings and superfluities of his incomprehensible sanctity. And history teaches us the same lesson.

Look at the Protestant countries which threw off all devotion to her three centuries ago, under the notion that to put her from their thoughts would be exalting the praises of her Son. Has that consequence really followed from their profane conduct towards her? Just the reverse—the countries, Germany, Switzerland, England, which so acted, have in great measure ceased to worship him, and have given up their belief in his divinity; while the Catholic Church, wherever she is to be found, adores Christ, as true God and true Man, as firmly as ever she did, and strange indeed would it be if it ever happened otherwise. Thus Mary is the Tower of David. (*Meditations and Devotions,* pp. 68–69.)

Virgin Most Powerful

THIS GREAT UNIVERSE, which we see by day and by night, or what is called the natural world, is ruled by fixed laws, which the Creator has imposed upon it, and by those wonderful laws is made secure against any substantial injury or loss. One portion of it may conflict with another, and there may be changes in it internally, but, viewed as a whole, it is adapted to stand forever. Hence the Psalmist says: "He has established the world, which shall not be moved."

Such is the world of nature; but there is another and still more wonderful world. There is a power which avails to alter and subdue this visible world, and to suspend and counteract its laws; that is, the world of angels and saints, of Holy Church and her children. And the weapon by which they master its laws is the power of prayer.

By prayer all this may be done, which by nature is impossible. Noah prayed, and God said that there never again should be a flood to drown the race of man. Moses prayed, and ten grievous plagues fell upon the land of Egypt. Joshua prayed, and the sun stood still. Samuel prayed, and thunder and rain came during the wheat harvest. Elias prayed, and brought down fire from heaven. Eliseus prayed, and the dead came to life. Ezekiel prayed, and the vast army of the Assyrians was smitten and perished.

This is why the Blessed Virgin is called powerful—nay, sometimes, all-powerful, because she has, more than anyone else, more than all angels and saints, this great, prevailing gift of prayer. No one has access to the Almighty as his Mother has; none has merit such as hers. Her Son will deny her nothing that she asks; and herein lies her power. While she defends the Church, neither height nor depth, neither men nor evil spirits, neither great monarchs, nor craft of man, nor popular violence can avail to harm us; for human life is short, but Mary reigns above, a queen forever. (*Meditations and Devotions*, pp. 70–71.)

Help of Christians

OUR GLORIOUS QUEEN, since her Assumption on high, has been the minister of numberless services to the elect people of God upon earth, and to his Holy Church. This title of "Help of Christians" relates to those services of which the Divine Office, while recording and referring to the occasion on which it was given her, recounts five, connecting them more or less with the Rosary.

The first was on the first institution of the devotion of the Rosary by St. Dominic, when, with the aid of the Blessed Virgin, he succeeded in arresting and overthrowing the formidable heresy of the Albigensians in the south of France.

The second was the great victory gained by the Christian fleet over the powerful Turkish Sultan in answer to the intercession of Pope St. Pius V, and the prayers of Rosary societies all over the Christian world. In lasting memory of this wonderful mercy, Pope Pius introduced her title *"Auxilium Christianorum"* [Help of Christians] into her Litany; and Pope Gregory XIII, who followed him, dedicated the first Sunday in October, the day of the victory, to our Lady of the Rosary.

The third was, in the words of the Divine Office, "the glorious victory won at Vienna, under the guardianship of the Blessed Virgin, over the most savage Sultan of the Turks, who was trampling on the necks of the Christians; in perpetual memory of which benefit Pope Innocent X dedicated the Sunday in the octave of her nativity as the feast of her august name."

The fourth instance of her aid was the victory over the innumerable force of the same Turks in Hungary on the Feast of St. Mary ad Nives, in answer to the solemn supplication of the confraternities of the Rosary; on occasion of which Popes Clement XI and Benedict XIII gave fresh honor and privilege to the devotion of the Rosary.

And the fifth was her restoration of the Pope's temporal power, at the beginning of this [nineteenth] century, after Napoleon the First, Emperor of the French, had taken it from the Holy See. On this occasion Pope Pius VII set apart May 24th, the day of this mercy, as the Feast of the *Help of Christians* for a perpetual thanksgiving. (*Meditations and Devotions,* pp. 72–73.)

Virgin Most Faithful

THIS IS ONE of the titles of the Blessed Virgin, which is especially hers from the time of her Assumption and glorious coronation at the right hand of her Divine Son. How it belongs to her will be plain by considering some of those other instances in which faithfulness is spoken of in Holy Scripture.

The word "faithfulness" means loyalty to a superior, or exactness in fulfilling an engagement. In the latter sense it is applied even to Almighty God himself who, in his great love for us, has vouchsafed to limit his own power in action by his word of promise and his covenant with his creatures. He has given his word that, if we will take him for our portion and put ourselves into his hands, he will guide us through all trials and temptations and bring us safe to heaven. And to encourage and inspire us, he reminds us, in various passages of Scripture, that he is the faithful God, the faithful Creator.

And so, his true saints and servants have the special title of "Faithful," as being true to him as he is to them; as being simply obedient to his will, zealous for his honor, observant of the sacred interests which he has committed to their keeping. Thus Abraham is called the Faithful; Moses is declared to be faithful in all his house; David, on this account, is called the "man after God's own heart"; St. Paul returns thanks that "God accounted him faithful"; and, at the last day, God will say to all those who have employed their talents well, "Well done, good and faithful servant."

Mary, in like manner, is preeminently faithful to her Lord and Son. Let no one for an instant suppose that she is not supremely zealous for his honor, or, as those who are not Catholics fancy, that to exalt her is to be unfaithful to him. Her true servants are still more truly his. Well as she rewards her friends, she would deem him no friend, but a traitor, who preferred herself to him. As he is zealous for her honor, so is she for his. He is the Fount of Grace, and all her gifts are from his goodness. O Mary, teach us ever to worship thy Son as the One Creator, and to be devout to thee as the most highly favored of creatures. (*Meditations and Devotions*, pp. 74–75.)

Morning Star/Star of the Sea

1.

WHAT IS THE nearest approach in the way of symbols, in this world of sight and sense, to represent to us the glories of that higher world which is beyond our bodily perceptions? What are the truest tokens and promises here, poor though they may be, of what one day we hope to see hereafter, as being beautiful and rare? Whatever they may be, surely the Blessed Mother of God may claim them as her own. And so it is; two of them are ascribed to her as her titles, in her Litany—the stars above, and flowers below. She is at once the *Rosa Mystica* [Mystical Rose] and the *Stella Matutina* [Morning Star].

And of these two, both of them well suited to her, the Morning Star becomes her best, and that for three reasons.

First, the rose belongs to this earth, but the star is placed in high heaven. Mary now has no part in this nether world. No change, no violence from fire, water, earth, or air affects the stars above; and they show themselves, ever bright and marvelous, in all regions of this globe, and to all the tribes of men.

And next, the rose has but a short life; its decay is as sure as it was graceful and fragrant in its noon. But Mary, like the stars, abides forever, as lustrous now as she was on the day of her Assumption; as pure and perfect, when her Son comes in judgment, as she is now.

Lastly, it is Mary's prerogative to be the morning star which heralds in the sun. She does not shine for herself, or from herself, but she is the reflection of her and our Redeemer, and she glorifies *him*. When she appears in the darkness, we know that he is close at hand. He is Alpha and Omega, the First and the Last, the Beginning and the End. Behold he comes quickly, and his reward is with him, to render to everyone according to his work. "Surely I come quickly. Amen. Come, Lord Jesus." (*Meditations and Devotions*, pp. 76–77.)

2.

TRULY ART THOU a star, O Mary! Our Lord indeed himself, Jesus Christ, he is the truest and chiefest star, the bright and morning star, as St. John calls him, that star which was foretold from the beginning as destined to rise out of Israel, and which was displayed in figure by the star which appeared to the wise men in the east.

But if the wise and learned and they who teach men in justice shall shine as stars forever and ever; if the angels of the churches are called stars in the hand of Christ; if he honored the apostles even in the days of their flesh by a title, calling them lights of the world, if even those angels who fell from heaven are called by the beloved disciple stars; if lastly all the saints in bliss are called stars, in that they are like stars differing from stars in glory; therefore most assuredly, without any derogation from the honor of our Lord, is Mary his Mother called the Star of the Sea, and the more so because even on her head she wears a crown of twelve stars. Jesus is the light of the world, illuminating every man who cometh into it, opening our eyes with the gift of faith, making souls luminous by his almighty grace. And Mary is the star, shining with the light of Jesus, fair as the moon, and special as the sun; the star of the heavens, which it is good to look upon; the star of the sea, which is welcome to the tempest-tossed, at whose smile the evil spirit flies, the passions are hushed, and peace is poured upon the soul.

Hail then, Star of the Sea, we joy in the recollection of thee. Pray for us ever at the throne of Grace; plead our cause, pray with us, present our prayers to thy Son and Lord—now and in the hour of death, Mary be thou our help. (*Meditations and Devotions*, pp. 87–88.)